Christian Vocation

Christian
Vocation

RENÉ VOILLAUME
translated by
ELIZABETH HAMILTON
With a concluding address by Pope Paul VI

Dimension Books · Denville, New Jersey

248

First American Edition
by Dimension Books Inc.

First published as
Retraite au Vatican
by Editions Fayard, Paris
This translation first published 1973 and
© *Darton, Longman & Todd Ltd, 1973*

ISBN 0 232 51204 3

Contents

1 Contemplation and Love of the Father with Jesus

Can there be bonds of love uniting God and man? Can there be a true loving relationship between God and his creature whom he has redeemed? Is it really possible?

When we listen to contemplatives such as Saint John of the Cross, Saint Teresa of Avila, Saint Francis of Assisi and, nearer our own times, Brother Charles of Jesus, and when we find that they are carried away by love of God, overflowing with joy, we cannot but ask what does this mean? Are they deluding themselves? When we read the ecstasies of Saint Catherine of Sienna, have we, here, a rare phenomenon? Or is this a reality which concerns ourselves? Can we dare to aspire to share in God's love in a like manner? Left to our own feeble efforts, we dare not and cannot face God, our Creator, in his eternal silence. Only in Jesus can we learn about eternal love, hidden in the bosom of the Father before time began. Jesus manifests love to us: 'Father, you loved me before the creation of the world.' 'As the Father loved me, I have loved you, and I abide in his love.'

There are no elaborate discourses. Jesus simply allows it to be apparent that he is loved and that he loves in return. In words of extraordinary simplicity he reveals the mystery, hidden in God from all eternity, of the loving relationship between the Father and the Son.

Jesus reveals also the eternal love which is extended to us. For we, as sons of God by adoption, are drawn after

Jesus into this relationship of love. 'As the Father has loved me, so I have loved you.' He goes on to prove this. We have only to follow Jesus, step by step, through the Gospel. We see the heart of the Saviour, the heart of the shepherd of souls, revealing itself at every moment with delicacy, tenderness, and a boundless respect for the poor and for sinners.

We should read again the parables of the prodigal son and the lost sheep. They are extraordinary. We are perhaps too used to these texts and their content. I remember a Moslem from Tunis, a professor at the Grand Mosque, whom the White Fathers had asked to translate into Arabic the Gospel story of the prodigal son. This Moslem was a religious man, deeply sensitive to the transcendence of God. When he brought his translation he wept as he read it: he had not imagined that God could feel such tenderness for men.

Then there is the love of Jesus for the rich young man: 'Jesus looked at him, and loved him.' There is also his prolonged conversation with the woman of Samaria: we feel close to this woman for whose sake he takes the trouble to explain so much, revealing to her, it seems, his mission. There is the way he behaves to the woman taken in adultery. There is Lazarus, his friend, over whom he weeps.

Yet all these manifestations of the love of Jesus are restrained. They are as simple as they are hidden. How many persons have really understood the meaning of these parables? Among those who went with Jesus from place to place, who saw his miracles, who saw him weep, how many were there who really understood? It is characteristic, it seems, of the revelation of God that it is so restrained, so simple, that only hearts enlightened by the Holy Spirit can hear it or understand it. 'Those who have ears to hear, let them hear.' Yet Jesus gives to men the greatest possible sign of love: 'No one has greater love than this, that he lay down his life for his friends.' And: 'Jesus having loved his own who were in the world, loved them to the end': he died for them.

As to ourselves, individually, do we really believe in the love of the Lord? We must ask this question. It is not so much a matter of our being convinced that God sent his Son to save the world – we believe this in a general kind of way: we believe that the Lord loves the world and all mankind. It is a question, rather, of being convinced that we are loved as persons. It is more difficult than is generally supposed to believe that we are loved: that we are the object of an immense love. It is more difficult perhaps to believe this than to believe in our love for the Lord. It is more difficult to know that we are loved than to love. On the spiritual road many Christians become despondent and weary simply because they do not know that they are loved.

What we are told about the saints shows that for them everything begins with the discovery, the certainty, that they are loved by God. Saint Thérèse of Lisieux could not endure the thought of not being the most beloved of the Lord; she knew herself loved, preferred even, before all! These souls have a kind of jealousy. They want God totally, as though for themselves alone: they want to be loved by God with all the love that is his.

Why, then, is it difficult for us to believe in love? Some of the difficulties stem from the imagination. We think of all the human beings who exist and have existed: we are lost – swamped, as it were, in a mass of persons. We speak more and more of crowds, masses. Jesus himself addressed the crowds. How can there be personal relations? It seems unlikely, impossible. And yet God is simple. God is so simple that he cannot be divided. Where God is, he is there in his entirety. Where there is God's love, there is the whole of God's love. We cannot be loved by God 'by half' or 'a little'. We cannot enjoy a fragment of the Lord's love: this is not possible. The love of God is indivisible. The reality of God which is granted to us is granted to each one in its entirety. Faith and reflection on the nature of God should, then, convince us that it is not an illusion, not a figment of the imagination, if we feel sure, when we withdraw into solitude, that God in his love is with us in his entirety. Don't we get this impression when we read the conversations between Catherine of Sienna and her Lord? One would suppose that the Lord had nothing to do in this world except to concern himself with Catherine!

Yes, if we really want to come closer to the Lord, we must begin by believing that we are loved. We must ask for this grace. In the presence of God we must not be like those unfortunate children who have not been given enough love. They are immature and they have complexes because they have been deprived of love. In the spiritual life we need the health of soul which comes from the knowledge that we are loved indefectibly, perpetually, wholly, with all the love of Christ. We must believe, then, in love. We must believe, and not be put off by a sense of our unworthiness. There are, of course, times in our lives when we feel a sort of disgust with ourselves, when we ask how we can be an object of interest. 'How can God be interested in me? How can he really love me?' 'I shall love him and manifest myself to him,' Jesus said. 'I shall manifest myself to him.' How does he manifest himself? Here we are confronted with a mystery. In the response of love that we give to the Lord we need to realize, at least sometimes, that we are loved by him. We feel this only rarely. But then it is a question of faith, not feelings.

But how do we respond to the love of the Lord? This is a further problem. For to love God is not the same as to love a human being. To love the Lord, even if we believe he is our brother, our friend, is not the same as loving a human being who is a brother or a friend. For us, the word 'love' evokes a feeling that we experience towards other human beings. By our very nature we have no experience of a different form of love. That is why love of God is difficult to understand, and we are clumsy in our efforts to love him.

What does it mean, then, to love Jesus? We should follow the road taken by all who have been called by God. Many, undoubtedly, have experienced on this road graces that are usually called 'consolations' – graces, that is, that make an emotional impact. This, I think, is usual at an early stage. If we consider the Apostles and their Master, we find something similar. At the beginning the Apostles are full of enthusiasm, ready for everything. When Jesus asks the sons of Zebedee: 'Can you drink the chalice that I must drink?' they answer without hesitation that they can. And as the Passion draws near and they feel, in a confused kind of way, that something serious is going to happen to their Master, Peter does not want to hear about this. And when Jesus wants it to be understood that Peter cannot follow him where he is going, Peter says: 'How do you mean? Why can't I follow you? I would give my life for you.' But Jesus replies: 'You will give your life for me? Truly, I tell you, before the cock crows you will have denied me three times.' Peter replied with still greater insistence: 'Though I were to die with you, even so I would not deny you?' We have all of us known this: the enthusiasm, the confidence, we feel at the beginning. We have not yet measured the true situation; we do not yet know what it means to love the Lord.

Our love of the Lord is not only unique by its very nature and by reason of its own laws – in that it is directed to God. It is also a love which makes us travel by unexpected paths: those which lead to the cross. The Apostles all had to pass that way. 'A cock crowed and the Lord, turning, looked at Peter, and Peter went out and wept bitterly.' Here we have the story of each one of us. But the Lord knows this well. Yet it did not deter him from choosing Peter to be the foundation of the building, the one who, more than any other, would represent and symbolize in his Church, constancy, fidelity, and strength. We have to discover little by little that it is not feelings nor a natural, spontaneous generosity which will take us far on the way to the Lord. Jesus has warned us of this.

What, I ask once more, does it mean to love? 'If you love me you will keep my commandments. He who receives my commandments and keeps them, he it is who loves me.' We find this prospect, it must be admitted, a little daunting. Is to love God, then, the carrying out of a duty? Is it simply obedience to a law? Does it mean no more than a cold fidelity to commandments? Many priests and religious, having heard the call of the Lord and responded to it, are troubled by a feeling of this kind. Is to love Jesus a duty? Then, again, many have the impression that they have not, in fact, encountered anyone to love. Some are, so to speak, numbed. They try to be faithful (perhaps to a heroic degree) to the demands of a law: the law of Jesus, the law of the Gospel. But there is something in them which has not fully opened: they have not encountered Jesus.

Then we ask: What ultimately does it mean to encounter Jesus in our lives? Is it a question of feelings? Is it something experienced on the level of the emotions? No, for we are well aware how Jesus said that to love him was to do his will. Moreover, he showed that his love for his Father was of this kind: 'If you keep my commandments, you will abide in my love, even as I have kept the commandments of my Father and abide in his love.' Now, this is assuredly true; for the perfection to which we have been called, and the love to which we ought to give expression in our lives and on which we shall be judged on the last day, means doing the Lord's will and keeping his commandments. Yet something more is needed. The object of our love is the Lord himself, and so the love we feel for God, the love we feel for Jesus Christ, must without question be accompanied either by contemplation or by a deep tenderness for men.

This is the way in which the Lord leads us beyond ourselves. In other words, I do not think that, in our love for Jesus, we could get beyond the first stages, where the senses and emotions are involved, without being guided by the Holy Spirit, and this action of the Holy Spirit will find expression either through the graces of contemplation or the graces of a tenderness which enable us to give ourselves wholly to our neighbour. We must, I believe, follow one of these two ways. If we do so, we shall know what the love of God really means: Hermits and contemplatives, though they may live in the desert without contact with their fellow men, know the meaning of God's love; they are overwhelmed with the happiness of serving him; the joy of being in his presence; the peace which only the Lord gives and is alone able to give; for a joy and a peace of this kind remain in us, despite the Cross, despite difficulties, despite weaknesses.

And that is why the saints of whom we have spoken are able – either by contemplation and prayer or else by a total surrender to the service of others – to persevere in fidelity in their love of the Lord. And they do so in the darkness of faith: a darkness that lasts and at the end perhaps becomes even more complete, more distressing. For it is a darkness which is really only enlightened from within, by the Lord's own light, which transcends human consciousness.

Brother Charles of Jesus experienced both these paths of love: contemplation (he spent hours of his life simply 'looking at' the Lord) and tenderness showered upon mankind, for he was entirely devoted to the poor. Nevertheless he wrote towards the end of his life: 'I hang on to faith; I don't know any more whether I love God, and I don't know any more whether he loves me: he has never told me so.' Such is the reality of the spiritual life. And yet, in this night of darkness, you know that you belong to the Lord; that, despite all, you are responding to his love and are deeply loved by him.

2 Prayer with Jesus

We are going to reflect on prayer. Why should we pray? In the world as it is today, we can pray only if we believe in the value of prayer. In the first place we think of prayer as something difficult and there are plenty of objections to put us off. Is prayer really necessary for us? We do not feel, all that much, a psychological need for prayer. We can live without it. Indeed we can even find sometimes that the worth of persons, even their moral worth, is not always in relation to whether they pray or do not pray. If there is something for which we feel the need, it is, rather, leisure – leisure to recollect ourselves in peace and silence. But that is not prayer, or not necessarily so. Anyway, have we time to pray? As soon as we break off our activities in order to pray, we immediately feel pressed by things waiting to be done. We have to help our neighbour or carry out some duty. And so we hurry back to take up our tasks again. And the greater our responsibilities and the wider their range, and the more involved we are in the complexities of our social relationships, so much the more does time for prayer diminish, indeed vanish. And we do not feel guilty, for we think that, after all, it is better to devote ourselves to others than to cease from our activities – particularly as nothing stops us from remaining united to God during our occupations. Provided we think of God now and again, why give special time to prayer? Besides, do we not find in the Gospel a justification for this attitude? Has not Jesus said: 'It is not those who say, "Lord, Lord," but those who do the will of my Father who enter into the Kingdom of Heaven.' We have the impression, then, that in carrying out our duties faithfully, in striving after perfection in charity, we live in conformity with the will of God. Moreover has not Jesus said that the Father knows what we need before we ask him and that it is pointless, therefore, to pile up words? And so we are more and more content with what today is usually called 'the prayer of diffusion' and, since we are praying all the time, we no longer have the need to devote definite moments to prayer.

Besides, the liturgical reform and the need strongly felt for a kind of community prayer that will express our 'togetherness' and our fellowship one with another in the sight of God and thus unite us in the presence of the Lord – does not this need, which is a genuine one, suffice? Why look for anything else?

The necessity of praying to God with the purpose of obtaining from him something for which we have need – this makes itself felt less and less in the present climate of thought, and the reasons are obvious. If the things we ask from God depend not on man but on the laws of nature, then what is the point of asking? Why pray for rain, if the meteorological forecasts predict drought? It is certainly not worth while. God has made the laws of nature and it is to be expected that these should produce their effects. If, on the other hand, what we ask for depends on man, why pray? Would it not be better to make up our minds to bring about these things, instead of asking God to do so for us? The attitude which disposes man to take refuge in prayer is surely dependent on an outdated conception of the working of Providence, as if God intervened to make things happen without their passing through the secondary causes which he has himself ordained. Obviously it is more sensible to take hygenic measures to prevent the spread of an epidemic than to pray that the epidemic may not spread. We find ourselves, then, faced with a psychological change in man's thinking in the matter of prayer. All forms of prayer are questioned, except perhaps communal prayer – and one can't help asking at least in certain cases, whether this kind of prayer is valid as such and is not simply an expression of fellowship.

*

We must, first and foremost, consider Jesus, for if we remain on the level of psychological and human reactions we will not find a solution to the question of prayer.

Jesus in contemplation prayed to his Father. I am not speaking of the attitude which as a Jew he would have taken in regard to participation in the prayers in the synagogue and the punctilious observance of the feasts in the Temple. I am concerned with the unique, entirely personal prayer which took place between himself and his Father. If we consider the Gospel as a whole, it is clear that the prayer of the Lord is continual, authentic, genuine: that it is the expression – in the human intelligence and the human heart of Jesus – of the eternal dialogue of love and contemplation exchanged between the persons of the Trinity before time began. The whole human race is caught up into this dialogue. It is a great mystery. Divine things are, I have said, simple. And the life of the Son of God, in the person of Jesus, is simple. It is hidden by its very simplicity, and yet it is totally genuine. Moreover we see its brightness shining from within. The Gospel has preserved for us a few of these manifestations of the prayer of Jesus.

It began when he was twelve years old. Who could say what it must have meant to this child – for he was indeed a child – to awaken, in his human consciousness, to the unique relationship existing between him, the eternal Son, and his Father? It was so secret that his mother hardly suspected anything. The reply Jesus gave to his parents – 'Did you not know that I must be busy with my Father's affairs?' –

bewildered them: they did not fully understand what he meant. It was in the depths of this child's soul that began that extraordinary dialogue. He was occupied with the concerns of his Father. Later, when Jesus was baptized, it was while he was in prayer that the Holy Spirit came down on him. While he was in prayer. We cannot imagine what those forty days in the desert meant to Jesus, when, in the prime of life, he was alone, face to face with his Father. His human intelligence, his human heart, were wholly occupied with the contemplation of his Father, with the concerns of his Father. The concerns, of his Father meant, first and foremost, the redemption of the world; that is the Passion. During the months that followed, Jesus often withdrew to a place apart to pray. This seems to have been habitual. Thus, he spent nights in desert places. Yes, it is impossible to imagine what transpired in his soul. It is, however, after one of these periods of withdrawal that Jesus, at the request of his disciples, formulated the prayer we call the *Our Father*. We have only to take its phrases one by one – above all in the first part – to have an idea of how Christ prayed.

Jesus prayed before choosing his Apostles: he prayed that the faith of Peter might not fail. We need only read his prayer in the Gospel of Saint John, after the Last Supper, to realize what must have been the intentions of Christ in prayer. And these are mere glimpses, granted to the Apostles, of what the prayer of Christ must have been in all its depth. He was praying when he was transfigured on Mount Tabor. It was as though the impact made by his contemplation of the Father could not be contained within him: the glory shone through his entire human body. It was not yet his glorification in the full sense of the word, yet, as the eternal Son, Jesus aspired to this and so begged his Father to glorify him. And again, there was the time when Philip and Andrew went to find him, to bring to him some Greeks. Jesus cried aloud before the crowd;

B

'Now my soul is troubled.' His words explain: 'Unless the grain falls to the earth and dies, it bears no fruit.' He knew that it was he himself who must fall to the ground and die. 'Father glorify your Son in your presence.' This was the cry sent up in his prayer. We are conscious of the permanent quality of the prayer throughout the predictions of the Passion, during the last months of his time on earth. The cry that escaped him before the crowd was but a brief manifestation of an abiding relationship between Jesus and the Father.

Gethsemane was the culmination of the prayer of Christ. The disciples were there. Jesus asked them to pray: 'Watch and pray.' But it was beyond their power: they did not yet know how to pray. And then the cries of Jesus, as he was dying on the cross, were prayers. Only the Holy Spirit can help us to penetrate the mystery of Christ's unceasing prayer. In that Jesus was the Son, his prayer was unceasing, uninterrupted. As man, however, he devoted special times to prayer.

So much for what the Lord teaches us through his own life. However, in that we are the adopted sons of the Father, in that we are the brothers of Christ, redeemed and saved by him, we need to know whether we should follow the example of Christ – whether we should pray as Christ prayed. If we consider all those men and women who have been called to follow Christ more closely, we find that they have devoted themselves to prayer. We find, also, that they have not all done this in the same manner, which suggests that there are many kinds of vocation to prayer. But there is, nevertheless, first and foremost, the vocation to be a Christian: and we have to ask ourselves if this, in itself, does not carry with it a call, a special vocation to prayer. Then, having contemplated the prayer of Christ, we must reflect why and how, in following Jesus, we ought to pray.

*

We must ask ourselves about prayer as an obligation for a Christian. The answer of theologians and moralists who try to define what form the duty of prayer should take is by no means precise. When should we pray? How much time should we give to prayer? Some go to the lengths of asking how many times a year a Christian is under an obligation to pray.

To try to define the duty of prayer on the level of a moral obligation cannot satisfy us. Why? Because we cannot define in terms of this kind the demand of love which makes a child want to look at his Father, speak to his Father. 'If you wish,' Christ says to us. If you wish: it is, then, a question of love. Certainly we can be satisfied with little prayer in our lives. This is true of many Christians, even priests. Prayer is a demand of love, but it is not a psychological need. That is why we must be careful how we speak of this need of prayer. Perhaps we are too glib in telling Christians that they cannot live without prayer, when, in fact, they get on very well without it and in many instances feel no need of it. No, this demand belongs to the supernatural plane. We cannot say to God: 'Father,' except in the Holy Spirit.

The basic difficulty we experience as to the need of prayer lies in the fact that we have to begin to pray, if we are to feel deeply the need of it. Either we behave towards God as loving sons and therefore feel the need to look at our Father, love him, and tell him this, intimately, in secret; or else we resign ourselves to observe the law and obey the commandments, in which case we are no longer sons but merely faithful servants. Yet God wants more for us than that. 'I have not called you any longer servants, but friends.' Prayer, as a need and expression of love, involves much which cannot be defined, because we cannot define the content of love. But, this apart, is there not the duty of adoration?

*

Can the duty of a creature to adore God, be felt as a vital need? There is a commandment which says: 'You shall adore the Lord your God.' But we are entitled to ask what, here, does the word 'adore' mean? Does it mean a prayer of adoration or is it simply unclouded faith in the transcendence of God? Besides, adoration is not an attitude easily understood. Few Christians today grasp its significance. Even among priests, how many are there who really know the meaning of the expression to adore? Why? Because adoration is the supreme act directed to the Creator as such: it expresses an awareness of being a creature wholly dependent on his Creator, his Master. It is the cry of relative being in the face of absolute being, without which created being is nothing. Now modern man – for a number of reasons – has difficulty in putting himself on this level. There is indeed in the heart of man – perhaps to this extent for the first time in history – a deliberate and total rejection of the idea of dependence. He has come to regard the attitude that results from dependence as a defect: a surrendering of self. He has adopted a new approach. Mastery over himself, his evolution, and his destiny, have become his ideal. That is why, all too often, even those who continue to use the word 'adoration' no longer know what it really signifies. A Christian ought to understand what it means to adore his God. Adoration implies thanksgiving: a sense of wonder in the presence of God, the contemplation of God's beauty, and the prayer that his kingdom may come and his will be done

Another motive of prayer is the need to ask, to intercede, to cry aloud to God our sufferings and our distress. The psalms are perhaps the most perfect anthology of all the most primitive and spontaneous cries sent up by man to God. They include appeals for vengeance. But these cries are authentic. Man is expressing himself as he is – suffering, crushed, and scandalized by injustice.

Intercession at its highest is that of Jesus. It alone is

effective, and that is why every true prayer of intercession participates in the prayer of Christ. But we must consider more closely the prayer of petition, if we are to answer the objections raised previously. It must, however, be said that the prayer of petition was taught us by Jesus himself. When Jesus speaks to us about prayer it is almost always the prayer of petition: 'Ask and you will receive'. The parables of the importunate friend and the widow who importunes the judge are examples.

But why ask, when the Lord knows what we need? Should we first count on our own efforts to procure the things which we want? Or should we be aware of our powerlessness to obtain them – even to the point of fostering this feeling of powerlessness, so as to make our prayer of petition more urgent, more real? 'Lord, I look only to you for this.' And should we hold on to this feeling of dependence, confronted as we all are, on the one hand by an increasing awareness of the inevitability of the laws of nature, on the other by the concept that man is responsible for shaping his own destiny. We must agree that there can be, in our way of speaking about prayer, traces which suggest that we do not take into account these two realitites. We must be on our guard. The way we pray cannot remain static, if we accept all that is true in the development of man in relation to these two points. The attitude of modern man is characterised by a greater awareness of the exactitude with which the laws of nature function. He knows why there are earth tremors, why there are cyclones, why epidemics spread. He knows it will become more and more possible to foresee these or to overcome them. He knows this will be the only real way by which he can protect himself from them. Everyone will agree that it is more realistic and more efficacious to know in advance that a cyclone is on the way and therefore take shelter, than it is to recite litanies asking God to protect us from these natural disasters. We must recognize that there is truth in this, and realize that a change in the outlook of man is inevitable. In itself this change is not always for the worse: it is in fact good and to be expected.

Again, is it a bad thing that man should be more aware of his responsibilities as to his own evolution?

There is in our times, as you know, a widely accepted ideology which stems from a deterministic concept of history. Now the strange thing is that the persons and societies soaked in this ideology, instead of behaving in a deterministic manner – that is, submitting passively to events – are found, on the contrary, to be among the most active and dynamic in trying to break this determinism, as if the latter found expression through them and through the dynamism of their human activity. Moreover we christians, who reject this determinism, who believe in the freedom of man's will, appear less dynamic. Are we entitled, for instance, to talk about taking refuge in prayer? It is an expression sometimes used, but we should be careful, for it can be wrongly interpreted. We do not seek refuge in prayer as though we were running away from our responsibility to take action, or as if we doubted the efficacy of action. In my opinion the prayer of petition should remain in the hearts of christians as strong and as deep as ever, but perhaps the nature of the demand should be modified. Do we pray for peace? But can we sincerely pray for peace if at the same time we are not doing everything in our power (and even more), using in fact all our energy to bring peace about? That is the problem. We must be careful not to give the impression, when speaking about prayer, that we are opting out of our responsibilities as human beings, as if God, alone, should rescue us.

Others will reply: No, whether there is peace or war depends on mankind. And this is true: they are right. But we know also – and this is the tragedy of our world today – that men are the victims of a determinism in events and an unleashing of powers: a situation which they have themselves more or less provoked or even organized. There is the power of technology, the power of a complicated economic system. But, even so, it is possible for men, if they wish, to modify this kind of servitude. A great flood of prayer should, I believe, rise from our hearts, not asking God to give us peace, but rather that we may have the vision, the courage, and the capacity to work to establish peace. For if there is in the world a mystery which no science, no sociology, no economic law can penetrate, no statistics calculate, it is the freedom of man's will. And it is at this depth that the mystery of divine action and grace come into play, and, in the last analysis, our destiny is decided. We need light to enlighten the intelligence, strength to sustain the will, courage to be capable of detachment, and a sincere, disinterested love of others. But in the end it will be men who will bring about peace or war. Perhaps we do not make this sufficiently clear to our fellow Christians. Hence the reaction of some who, when asked to pray for peace, reply: 'No, we must work for peace, not pray for it.' And we have to admit that sometimes we do not adequately relate prayer to man's responsibilities. I know that we are touching here upon the unfathomable mystery of God's government and man's freedom. But for that very reason we must not over-simplify the problem.

A last question. Can the Christian be satisfied with liturgical or communal prayer? Clearly this problem poses another that is deeper: the relation of the individual to the community. In society it is more and more evident that we need the fellowship of others, if we ourselves are to develop. Man cannot get along – and he will be able to do so less and less – without society. This is true on all planes: intellectual, cultural, economic. And he will become increasingly dependent. This is man's dilemma. For he discovers that he cannot to without home, intimate relationships, friendships, since it is on this level that he feels fully a person. Yet those who possess the Christian hope know that, at the end, they will each be alone before God. Each one of us dies alone. And it is then that each will be fully aware of his own responsibilities, and the person attain his unique fulfilment. Then we will know what it really means to be a person created in the image of God. Meanwhile, in the world as it is, we have not yet found the balance between our demands as persons and those of a communal life. And as life in religion of necessity reflects our lives as men – seeing that the supernatural builds on the natural without destroying it – there are, on the plane of Christian prayer, repercussions of this same problem concerning relations between the community and a personal life.

We must, then, take into account what is required as to our relationship, as individuals, with the Lord. Christ is certainly not to be thought of in terms of a body of which we are anonymously the members – members and nothing more. Are we going to be saved collectively, all together? In the Body of Christ we are, indeed, interdependent one upon the other. But ultimately we are, nevertheless, the friends of Jesus, the brothers of Jesus, children of one Father. And we are this as persons, with all the legitimate demands that devolve from it. The Christian life must, in so far as prayer is concerned, strike a balance between the liturgical life (or prayer in community) and the growth of an individual, intimate, prayer without which there can be no real Christian perfection – no growth of the spiritual life for man as a person.

It remains for us to consider, in practical terms, how to pray.

3 Prayer with Jesus
(continued)

Personal prayer – for that is the kind of prayer of which I am thinking at present – is the activity which best enables us to encounter God here on earth, and to converse with him. It employs, indeed, faculties which are, in us, the reflection – or I could call it the imprint or seal – of the divine image: namely, the intelligence and the will. And so in looking for a definition of prayer I come back to the simple words of Brother Charles of Jesus, which are, I think, for general usage, the best definition, as well as being the most complete and the one most likely to be within the grasp of all. To pray, he says, is to think of God and at the same time to love him. Everyone can understand what this means. Moreover it has the advantage that it allows us to set what we call prayer in the context of the two activities of man in which it is, as it were, encased: thought and love. In short, to think of God without at the same time showing our love for him in action (I am not of course excluding habitual love) amounts to reflection or meditation, which can be the study of theology. In the same way what we do for love or the service of our neighbour, when motivated by the charity of Christ who is within us, is certainly an act of charity uniting us to God, but it is not really prayer if at the same time we do not think explicitly of God. People sometimes confuse meditation and prayer, and at other times speak of 'diffused' prayer, when in reality they are talking of action inspired by love. For there to be prayer, there must be both thought and love. Let me explain. Suppose I were reflecting on God or exercising my intelligence in the study of theology. If, as I did so, I became aware of a feeling of love for God, this would be prayer. Or suppose, in a spirit of friendship, I were doing some service for others or carrying out some duty. If, while I were occupied in this way, the thought of God came to me, then, again, I would be praying.

Before reflecting on how to pray we should approach the Lord as the Apostles approached him: 'Lord, teach us to pray.' It seems, according to the Gospel, that Saint John the Baptist had taught his disciples a way of prayer, but we do not know what it was.

Those who search the Gospels for a method of prayer, or practical directives, are often disappointed. The Lord, in replying to the question put by the Apostles, thought it enough to give them the *Our Father*. But there are in the Gospel other teachings on the subject of prayer, and these I shall try to summarize.

Certain of these concern the attitude that is necessary if we are to pray. First of all we must be at peace with our fellow-men, for without charity we cannot be in the right disposition to pray. We must be at peace both with God and our brothers.

There is also humility. One of the most moving parables is that of the Pharisee and the tax collector. To understand its meaning we must rid ourselves of the idea that the Pharisees were a sect composed of hypocrites. No, the Pharisees, in general, were righteous, God-fearing men, anxious to carry out scrupulously the law of God in its entirety. The fault that the Lord finds in this particular Pharisee is simply that he is too conscious of his righteousness – that he knows he is righteous. If we are to draw near to God we would surely do better to put ourselves in the skin of the tax collector. The entire Gospel shows us that the Lord is drawn to this kind of person, that he prefers those who have humbly accepted their human frailties, and who are completely sincere in God's presence – totally aware of their plight as sinners. Their prayer then becomes deeply authentic: it is not posturing or a mere formality.

The Lord teaches us, too, not to be discouraged. And perhaps, there, we have his most important teaching on prayer. Again and again he tells us to persevere: numerous parables touch on this.

There is also confidence. We should pray as if we had already received an answer. We should be assured of the power of prayer – its power to be effective. The Lord fills out this teaching with other parables telling us that, if our petitions are always answered, it will not necessarily be in the way which we had in mind. We can conclude that in the prayer of petition the most important thing is not the plea for this or that, but the fact of asking: our attitude, too, when we ask – since this reveals how we stand in the sight of God. A Christian who cannot accept the condition of complete dependence on the Lord, which is required by the prayer of petition, does not, I think, fully realize what kind of person he ought to be.

Jesus opens for us the perspective of the action of the Holy Spirit in prayer. The Father will give the Holy Spirit to those who ask him, and Jesus adds these mysterious words 'He will come to those who love him, and manifest himself to them'.

Yes, the Lord has refused to give us what is called a method of prayer, although most people, including Christians, find the difficulties of prayer daunting – above all when they have a particular desire for it to be effective: for they would like to be conscious of their prayer during the act of praying; be sure that they are praying and praying well. We are touching here on perhaps the greatest difficulty in prayer. For when we are aware of having prayed well, we are satisfied with ourselves. Now, the prayer that is most perfect is often of a kind that eludes us, that we cannot grasp; it is an act which takes place in the depths of our being and defies comprehension. It is on this level that we experience at one and the same time the difficulty and the need in relation to methods of prayer.

I come, then, to these methods. There is a general feeling today that methods of prayer taught in the course of the last few hundred years have lost their efficacy. We must, therefore, consider what can be done to encourage prayer.

It is well to remember, first of all, that during prayer our inner activities of the highest order – those of recollection and contemplation of the divine mysteries – are united to the activity, entirely free and supernatural, of the Holy Spirit. It is essential to be clear about this. For either we forget the Holy Spirit or, because we do not believe in him, behave in a way that no longer allows him to function. This makes prayer an art at one and the same time difficult and simple; for it is one to which every human being, every Christian, is called. However, when we attempt to guide others in prayer, we ought to encourage a certain understanding of faith, a certain facility for recollection, a certain aptitude for meditation, for these are qualities that need to be developed and normally make the path to prayer easier. But what hope is there for those who are weighed down by fatigue, poverty, and overwork – those, too, who are not used to concentration, who have little intellectual culture? Is it conceivable that these, just because they are the poorest of all, should be deprived of true prayer? The very fact of putting this question shows us that ways of prayer differ from person to person; and that if we are entitled to demand a spiritual and theological training for those who are capable of it, and the use of these disciplines as a preparation for prayer, we cannot extend this demand to all. Let us remember the parable of the Pharisee and the tax collector. We should teach the ways of prayer to all, without exception, while taking into account the circumstances of each. Unhappily there are priests, responsible for the guidance of souls, who have not enough confidence in an ordinary Christian's capacity for prayer and contemplation.

Now, a word about how to pray. It is impossible to begin without preparation. We should recall the traditional methods of preparation – those, that is, which remain valid in our own times. Faith must be nourished. And faith can be nourished only by God's word and by a deepening of our understanding of his word. To devote ourselves to prayer without having nourished our faith is difficult, if not impossible. Besides, there would be something illogical in such an attitude. .

To pray well we should be in a state of charity. If we turn to God, seeking for light to know him better, this can be authentic only if we have the generosity to translate into action whatever this light enables us to see. We cannot deepen our understanding of the mystery of God if we are not ready to respond to the demands of love; to detach ourselves from things that pass. When we begin to pray we should be in a state of detachment from all that is not God. The complete stripping away of all things, as exemplified in Saint John of the Cross, appears to be a kind of reverbation in his soul of the contemplation of him who is the only true good. We must be conscious of the plenitude which the possession of God can give, if we are to be able to detach ourselves from all else. If we do not begin by putting ourselves in a wholly receptive frame of mind, and if we are not ready at least for a moment, at least during our time of prayer, to leave all for God – we are not ready for this, then we cannot penetrate into the heart of prayer. Someone has written that moments of pure prayer are indeed rare in the life of a man, but that these are accompanied by what can only be compared to that total stripping away of all things which will take place at death. What that means is clear. Let us be very humble and let us say that, whatever stage we have reached, it is worth while to persevere along the path of prayer, even if our moments of pure prayer – that is a genuine encounter with God – are rare. Besides, this perseverance accords with the words of our Lord: 'Ask and you will receive, knock and it will be opened to you.' There would be no need to ask someone to knock if the door were always immediately opened. To ask us to knock again and again, makes sense only if the door can remain closed for a long time. In view of the diversity of the gifts of the Spirit and the action of God on souls, some, even in the contemplative life, can be called by God to a humility and perseverance that amounts to waiting at the door, knocking without giving up. We are convinced it will be opened, but we cannot know at what moment nor how. Perhaps for some it will be only in the Beatific Vision; but then – we have God's assurance – for these the door will be wide open.

We have observed that traditional methods of prayer appear ineffective at the present time, for reasons that are purely psychological. Modern art aims at shapes which are restrained, devoid of unessentials, basic. Our contemporaries have a craving for simplicity. This is why simple ways of prayer prove more effective, and the most simple of all consists in going straight to the point – using, to help us to pray, merely a saying of our Lord in the Gospel. But it is still true that mental discipline and a capacity for recollection should be learnt, and this is not always easy.

Finally we must learn – for our own sakes and then to be able to teach others – how to go to meet the Holy Spirit, to encounter him. Yes, we must learn to encounter the Holy Spirit. If the Lord really dwells in the depths of our souls; if, already here on earth, we are moving towards our supernatural destiny, it is natural that there should be within us a depth which we cannot plumb. It is not easy to define the dilemma of Christians in this world. If prayer is the highest activity of the theological life – one which prepares us for the vision of God and is, as it were, an anticipation of what it will be like after the resurrection, when we possess the Beatific Vision – we must accept that there is a certain imbalance between the work the Holy Spirit has begun within us and our actual capacities. We should, however, be convinced that the grace bestowed by the Holy Spirit on the road of prayer is not reserved for a few saints, who are contemplatives and thought of as exceptions: 'The Father will give the Holy Spirit to those who ask him.' This means, unless I am mistaken, that the Holy Spirit will not come to those who do not desire this, who do not believe in his action, who do not thirst for what he alone can give.

To these remarks I should add, I feel, in closing, the elementary fact that we must have the courage to devote a certain amount of time to prayer. To offer our time to God is to offer him the first fruits of our activities: to acknowledge God's sovereignty over time. And this presupposes a sacrifice, in that the time thus given to God is taken away from, or sets a limit to, our human activities. We must, therefore, understand what is involved when we decide to consecrate definite time to prayer.

4 Prayer with Jesus
(continued)

To orientate our life of prayer and strike the necessary balance between action and contemplation, it is well to reflect for a moment on Christianity as it is today. In doing so we cannot fail to observe a kind of mutation in the life of prayer as lived by Christians. True, it does not concern a large number, but I have undoubtedly noticed among certain priests and nuns, as well as the laity, a working of the Holy Spirit which indicates a deepening awareness of prayer.

If a book were to be written about prayer as practised by Christians through the centuries, it could not fail to show how prayer has repeatedly been subject to change. Since the time when Saint Benedict took with him into the desert Christians who wanted to live inconditions favourable to a growth towards perfection, there has been, down to our own day, a gradual evolution. Slowly but surely, holiness in its highest form has been presented more and more as being within the scope of every Christian without distinction. It is only natural that things should not be static in the Body of Christ, and that, if there is an evolution, this should take the form of a deepening of the understanding. In all that concerns how we live and behave, in all that affects religion, there are factors which are bound to alter or disappear, in which case the evolution takes place through replacement and change. But when it is a question of basic values, the evolution can only come about through a deepening of the understanding and not by change. And this applies to prayer. If we go to the heart of prayer, into the souls of those who pray, things at that level can change only by the process of a deepening of understanding. Man to-day is exposed to a flood of influences which endanger the awareness and the growth of the person. Man is analysed, split up; he no longer can reach the centre of himself. The sciences which make a study of man do so from a variety of angles, and no one of these sciences can make a synthesis or reach the heart of the problem. Hence man runs the risk of losing his awareness of himself – what he is and the mystery that is his. There is, then, a growing need for a deepening of his awareness: he must strengthen himself in the sphere which is most important: his life with the Spirit.

We can no longer be content, as I shall explain, with short, quick prayers. Moreover the call to action is too urgent not to be included in the other demands of the Christian vocation. There is an appeal, indeed a demand, for this deepening of the life of prayer, which is another way of saying that the contemplative dimension of man must be better understood and become something of which we are more and more conscious. This is vital for every believer, every Christian. Faith is an invisible reality beyond the world we know must be intensified: it must be sufficiently alive to enable us to keep in contact with the world of God. Only at this cost can man grow and his action become fully effective, and this involves an awareness of a new dimension that is indispensable: the Christian dimension of love. Some (especially the young) when they speak of prayer, for which they feel the need in a confused sort of way, like to use the expression 'gratuitous' prayer. What do they mean by this? They mean prayer which is not intended to enrich us through meditation, nor, again, is it a demand for something. No, they have in mind a prayer for someone else, for God, a prayer that is wholly disinterested. This is what they feel the need for. Brother Charles of Jesus

C

speaks too – the expression is not in fact his own – of prayer which is a 'breathing out of self, a total forgetfulness of self, in the presence of God'. For a moment man's life is lost in God.

This need for basic prayer is matched by a lessening of interest in a superfluity of vocal prayers and what are called 'acts of piety'. Or else these vocal prayers must be restrained in expression and convey feelings that are genuine – the kind of thing one would want, oneself, to say to the Lord. There must be harmony between this vocal prayer and the attitude of those who use it. This tendency, far from being a set-back, seems rather a step forward in the deepening of prayer. Basically do we not, all of us, feel a need of this sort in our lives today? This 'essential' prayer – you will permit this word, though I could say prayer that is pure, 'absolute' in the methods it employs, one which involves in a much more serious manner the life of the person who practices it – this kind of prayer, is within the scope of our contemporaries and furthermore is indispensable.

I would like to give some instances not only because they are encouraging, but because they show in what direction the action of the Holy Spirit is moving, thus enabling us to listen to him the better.

I will give just two examples. The first is in Africa, in a Christian community made up of the poor. The only kind of prayer they knew, the only one that had been taught them, was participation in vocal prayers said together in church. One day one of the community, touched by the grace of God, began to discover the value of long, silent prayer. He stayed on in church, on his knees or sitting in his place, for nearly an hour after the service was over. This way of behaving appeared so unusual, so strange, that the priests thought the man could not be normal, that he must be unbalanced. But they came to realize what was happening in his soul. He was only a poor man, a worker, but he took the trouble to share his discovery with other Christians. At first there were three or four young couples, then ten, then twenty. In the end they constituted three or four groups. They used to pray in silence before the Blessed Sacrament and help each other to meditate on the Gospel.

The other example concerns some of the young who have a vocation to the religious life. It is indeed true that they seem unable to adapt to what we might call the spiritual exercises that usually divide the day in religious congregations – especially those founded during the last three centuries. Not only do the young not succeed in practising these forms of prayer, but prayers of this kind hardly ever produce any positive results in their spiritual life. I am speaking of the young with whom I have had dealings in the Fraternity. I do not speak for all, but the tendency is, I think, widespread. If, however, one knows how to direct these young men, I can testify that they have a thirst for prolonged prayer in a spirit of poverty – that they have, in fact, rediscovered the spirituality of the Desert Fathers. The 'absolute' quality of long periods passed in silence and solitude, under conditions of the utmost simplicity, prove to be extraordinarily beneficial. Generally speaking, I repeat, the young today are more at ease in the simple 'absolute' spirituality of the Desert Fathers, as distinct from the prayers and devotional practices usually associated with the religious life. A movement in this direction cannot fail to be the work of the Spirit. It would otherwise be impossible. Humanly speaking, no one would be capable of devoting himself to prolonged prayer without the action of the Holy Spirit.

We ourselves ought to take account of this, not only with a view to orientating our own personal prayer, but also for the sake of those – priests included – whom we have to direct. For what I have said of these young religious applies to many priests, namely, that today (and this is important) the necessary balance in the spiritual life – in the life of a

religious, in that of a priest – presupposes periods of prolonged prayer.

Time is needed if we are to pray; if we are to get down
into the depths of ourselves; if we are to enable the Holy
Spirit to help us, in poverty of heart, to attain detachment in
one form or another. Personal experience of God is essential
if we are to combat the increasing materialism of our day,
as well as the onslaughts made upon the intellectual and
philosophical foundations of our faith. It is vital, then, to
find time for prolonged prayer and we ought to help other
Christians, or at least some of them, to do the same.

*

This brings us to another point: the necessity of striking
a balance between action and contemplation – an alternating rhythm of activity and prayer.

What form should this rhythm take in life as it is lived
today? Experience in the spiritual direction of priests,
religious, and laity shows that it is practically impossible,
in modern life, to fit into each day all that is normally
regarded as being conducive to fostering in us a living
faith: meditation on the Scriptures, spiritual reading,
prayer. Pressures, distractions, exhaustion, nervous tension,
all combine to make it more difficult than formerly to pass
from action to recollection. And to do so takes longer.
I am convinced that this is the experience of many. We
need more time than in the past to recover peace of mind
and recollection in the spiritual life. Does not this fact
lead us to seek anew a rhythm conducive to relaxation and
a return to God – one, furthermore, which is profoundly
human? The society in which men live has always had its
repercussions on the religious life. Now, today, the balance
of our lives depends more than in the past on a marked
rhythm of rest and relaxation which is related to the week.
Week-ends are very important for relaxation, rest, and
leisure. Life would be unbearable without this rhythm.

Should we not have the courage to set aside for the Lord one day, or at least half a day, each week to be consecrated to meditation on the Scriptures, spiritual reading, and prolonged prayer? This would establish a true balance for the soul, which would thus find again peace and spiritual the relaxation.

We must stress the importance of a clearly defined monthly rhythm. Many of the clergy have found balance again in their priestly lives because they have been obliged to give a day a month to a retreat in a place other than the one where they normally carry out their duties.

There is also, it is well to recall, the traditional rhythm of the annual retreat. Those of the laity who manage to maintain, in the hurly-burly of everyday life, a truly generous Christian way of living, owe it often to the fact that every year they spend some days in retreat.

Moreover, among priests and religious there is a custom which is beginning to spread, whereby, after a period of some years in the ministry, one year is devoted to study, reflection, and genuine taking stock. This is sometimes called a sabbatical year and is roughly the equivalent of the 'refresher courses' which many of the professions are finding necessary in order to bring their knowledge up to date.

Weekly, monthly, and yearly retreats, as also the 'sabbatical' year, are what I call primary, indeed essential, means: they are not 'pious exercises'.

As to the 'exercises', this word can create confusion. To pray to the Lord cannot be called an exercise. If we visit a friend because we need his friendship, want to give him proof of ours and to enjoy his company, would we dream of calling this an exercise? The use of the word suggests an idea of relativity, whereas we are concerned with essential values – a genuine, vital act in our relationship with God. We cannot call this an exercise. That is what I meant when I spoke just now of the mutation which, in the spiritual life, should take the form of a deeper understanding of God. I observe, I think, in religious congregations a similar need, which shows itself in a craving for authenticity in our relations with God. Perhaps even the contemplatives need to become more truly contemplative. I recall one of the last conversations I had with Dom Sortais, Abbot-General of La Trappe, some months before his death, in which he told me that too much vocal prayer (likewise prayer in choir) had killed the contemplative life in some monasteries.

*

And now a word about the unity of our lives: the unity which should exist between action, contemplation, work, personal relationships, and prayer. Everyone should try to find unity in his life: it is a vital need. One of the questions most often put by priests and laity is: 'How can I find unity in my life?' There could be a danger in trying to establish an impossible psychological unity while, in so doing, sacrificing one of the two facets that give balance. Unfortunately, the one likely to be sacrificed is contemplation or prayer, for it is clearly impossible to dispense with action. Ought we, then, to abandon the idea of unity? Prayer and action each require conditions that, externally and psychologically, are different, if not irreconcilable: withdrawal versus the company of others, silence versus noise, solitude versus the crowd, recollection versus an outgoing concern. It is not within man's power to change these oppositions. Quite the contrary. The alternating rhythm of which we have spoken seems to be a law of man's nature. Even the Lord himself has set an example of submission to this law. He, too, used to go from the desert to the multitude, from the multitude to the desert. And he did so both as man and as the Son of God.

This alternation is, then, a law of mankind, a way of behaving that is wholly in conformity with man's nature.

We must not, therefore, try to resolve, on the psychological plane, this need for unity. It rests with each one of us to establish in his life – between this twofold vital need for contemplation and action – a balance that conforms to the duties of his state and, equally, to his spiritual calling in accordance with the action of the Holy Spirit.

But this rhythm, to the demands of which we should submit, does not involve any deep duality. For if the unity of our lives cannot be attained on the psychological plane, it is attainable at a deeper level: in the unity of love. It is, in fact, in our love of God, our love of Christ, that is established the unity between these periods given to God in solitude and those which we devote to the service of our brothers in Christ. This is a unity that disposes us to love, renouncement, and self-surrender.

And, then, apart from our dispositions and our acts, there is within us a movement towards the unity of which the Holy Spirit is the author. It is in our power to go to meet this work of the Holy Spirit, trying by regular prayer to foster a habit of thinking spontaneously of God in all circumstances and or orientating our actions towards him – through the purification and unity of our intentions. We should not, of course, continually beg God to reveal himself, strain ourselves to think of him at every moment. That would by to try to establish an impossible psychological union, which would end in imbalance, exhaustion, and nervous tension – specially in the religious life – whereas, on the contrary, we ought to attain a state of peace, inner relaxation, which is the fruit of being long in the company of the Lord through prayer. Above all, we ought to believe that the Holy Spirit, sent through Jesus, operates in us by his gifts at all times, not only at the moment of prayer, but in our activities. We should humbly and realistically accept our limitations both in prayer and in action. It rests with us to devote ourselves to prayer, to prepare ourselves for it, to begin to pray, and to advance as best we can, but we will come up against a limit beyond which only the Holy Spirit can enable us to pass. It is the same in action: we can indeed expend ourselves on a variety of activities, but we shall find our limitations in the strength we bring to them, in our courage and detachment and, above all, in the perfecting of our charity. Only the Holy Spirit can take us beyond these limitations. Whether in prayer or in action, we are, then, wholly dependent on the Spirit.

These few thoughts, most of which are the fruit of experience, can assure us, encourage us, and give us hope. However we are placed, it is within our capacity to grow in union with the Lord, for it depends on our establishing this rhythm of prayer and action, contemplation and activity, in which our lives will find not only its balance, but its possibility to grow in the grace of the Lord, under the guidance of the Holy Spirit.

5   Loving our Brothers with Jesus

We must learn how to love our brothers with Jesus. This precept to love our fellow men is at the same time the most gentle and reassuring of the commandments of Jesus, and yet the most serious, and one which sometimes fills us with dismay at the thought of its demands. We know, however, that without genuine brotherly love for men, there is no religion. This precept is the heart of religion. Even before the coming of Jesus, the imprecations of the prophets recalled that no sacrifices were pleasing to God, no form of worship possible, without humility of heart and justice in relation to our neighbour. We know, also, that this love for others is required of us by the world, by humanity: we feel a kind of nostaligia for this love and learn more and more that without love there is no possibility here on earth of our living at peace.

We must ponder, then, on the teachings of Jesus. As usual, these are extraordinarily simple and restrained. We have only to take two or three sayings of Christ and we have something to meditate on and work for until the end of the world: 'I give you a new commandment, that you love one another; that, even as I have loved you, so you also shall love one another.' That is all.

Why is this commandment new? A little before Jesus pronounced these words someone had asked him: 'What is the greatest commandment?' All Jesus did was to recall the law: 'You shall love the Lord your God with all your heart, with all your soul, with all your mind – this is the greatest and the first commandment. The second is likewise: You shall love your neighbour as yourself. On these two commandments hang all the law and the prophets. There is no commandment greater than these.' After reminding his listeners that in the ancient law it was written: 'You shall love your neighbour; you shall hate your enemy', 'An eye for an eye, a tooth for a tooth,' Jesus added: 'And I say to you: love your enemies; if someone strikes you on the left cheek, give him the right cheek.' But this is, so to speak, merely an application, a consequence. What is new is that the commandment to love one another means, henceforth, that we love our brothers as Jesus loves them. As the Incarnate Word loves men, we, henceforth, are obliged to love them in our turn. We have here the point of departure of a command that is without limit. What is new is the fact that the image of God, imprinted upon man, is now complete, brought to perfection. Man has become, over again, in a true sense, the son of God. Man cleansed in the blood of Christ, and having within him the image of the Lord, is a brother and member of Christ. All, then, is changed. Bonds are forged again between God and ourselves, between the Lord Jesus and ourselves; we are are become the brothers of Jesus, we have been redeemed by his blood. It is because these new bonds have been forged, because we are all, to some degree, involved, here on earth, in the love that is shared for all eternity by the Father and the Son, that we must love in conformity with this new relationship.

This same relationship in which we find ourselves means, in the first place, that we must look on men as Jesus looks on them. It is a question, then, of learning to determine what is the true good of men. What Jesus wants for men, we should want; what Jesus has done for men, we should do.

But there is another aspect of this commandment of the Lord, one which is often misunderstood, on which we ought to reflect for a moment. It is said in the commandment laid down by the law that we ought to love our neighbour 'as ourselves'. Now we are tempted to see in this directive what amounts to a watering down of our love for others; an excuse for what, in fact, is an ego-centric prudence. So we are not, then, obliged to love our brothers more than ourselves. We need not trouble too much about others, since it is justifiable to begin with self. We end up, therefore, with a philosophy of life that is indeed mediocre, and a conception wholly human, and even ego-centric, of the love of our neighbour. And yet the Lord repeated this commandment and seems, therefore, to underline its importance.

What does this mean? It is simply this: we are included within the charity that flows forth from the heart of Christ; we are loved by Christ. And if love is an outgoing of self, it is essential (if we are to understand its demands) to put ourselves within the heart of the Lord and reflect upon the manner in which he loves us and what he expects from us. As Jesus loves us, so we must love ourselves and desire for ourselves the good he desires for us. If love demands that we place ourselves within the heart of Christ, how can we fail to find there, above all, the love which he has for us? And so man is under an obligation to love himself as Jesus loves him. In that case there is no longer any problem: love is, indeed, an abandonment of self, and having abandoned self we should make our abode within the heart of Christ and, from there, learn to judge all things and to look upon ourselves. Yes, we have to live our lives, seeing ourselves from this point of view. Then we no longer have anything to fear, because, if we love ourselves as Christ loves us, it is no longer a question of some mediocre philosophy, but rather of a limitless demand. We find that in loving ourselves we have to demand of ourselves complete detachment and be ready, with Jesus, to go even to the length of dying for our brothers, since he died for us: 'A man has no greater love than this, that he lay down his life for his friends'. This means that the love we should have for ourselves depends on the measure of our imitation of Christ. Besides, all the saints have instinctively followed this path. Yes, we should love ourselves, but not in the way we think all too often. Moreover the Lord adds: 'That which you would have men do for you, do likewise for them.' In thus putting ourselves within the heart of Christ we cannot fail to desire to be loved by the Saviour, we cannot fail to desire to be saved wholly by him. And so we will be in a position to know what others are entitled to expect from us.

Thus there is established a mysterious unity between the heart of Christ, ourselves, and others. This close bond, this bond between the Lord, ourselves, and our brethren is, moreover, clearly expressed by the Lord himself: what we do for the least of our brothers, he tells us, we do for Christ. In the lives of the saints many episodes illustrate this truth. When Saint Francis kisses the leper he kisses Christ. There are, above all, the words of Saint John on which we should reflect: 'If we say that we love God whom we do not see, yet do not love our brothers whom we do see, then, indeed, we are liars.'

Why this parallel between God whom we canot see and our brother whom we can see? Our brother whom we can see is here, present. We know him. We are aware of his needs. We know what he is. He is there always, as it were, questioning our charity, reproaching us if we do not love him. Besides, he will not cease to demand this love from us, just as he will demand from us that we act with justice to him. We cannot, then, forget this plea to love our brothers nor have any illusions about it.

And yet to love God is another matter. In the first place how do we know that we love him? Because we experience some feelings deep within us? Because we are faithful to a few hours of prayer more or less without distractions? Or, again, because from time to time we make some sacrifices for him? What does this amount to in the sight of God? Is this really to love God? Do we really give him proof of our love? Can we say that we have abandoned self? We can be deluded in all this, for God keeps silence. God demands nothing from us. God asks nothing. And so we can persist in our illusions – believe we love God with all our heart, be full of good intentions. This is what gives an over-riding importance to the bond between God and man, as the object of our love, and this bond is infinitely more real than we think. One of the discoveries we shall make in the vision of God is to perceive this mysterious bond which exists between an individual human being and the Word made Flesh. Christ is man, and there is this close bond between each man and Christ. We should be on our guard against thinking of people· *en masse*, collectively. Christ is a man. And each man has a likeness to the Lord – is bound closely to him. We cannot approach the Lord without loving men as unique persons. We cannot love God without loving our brothers.

There is a parable of the Lord – one of the most beautiful and undoubtedly one of the most serious – which sets everything in the light of love. It is a vision of the Last Judgement, when, in the presence of God, whole nations, indeed all mankind, are assembled and a choice is made: a separation. There are those who have conformed to the will of God, those who have loved God – for it is the capacity to love which enables them to enjoy the vision of God and penetrate his mystery. There are those, too, who have been rejected because they cannot endure that God should look upon them, nor can they look him in the face, to love him. So, then, we shall be judged on the love we have shown our brothers. 'I was hungry,' Christ says, 'and you gave me to eat; I was thirsty, and you gave me to drink; I was homeless, and you took me in; naked, and you clothed me; sick, and you visited me; in prison, and you came to me.' And those who visited the hungry, the thirsty, prisoners, and the naked, say in astonishment: 'When, Lord, did we see you?' And Christ answers: 'Whenever you did this to the least of

my brothers, you did it to me.' This enumeration of the
thirst, the need, the wretchedness of men was, at the time
of our Lord, complete. Today we could add to it (that the
parable may remain authentic) the thirst for respect, the
thirst for education, the thirst for freedom, the thirst for
work – all those things, in fact, which men need if they are
to be, in the full sense, men. Let us grasp, then, the serious-
ness of this parable. We shall be judged on our love: not
our love in the sense of feelings, not words of love but on
love that is put into practice.

This teaching of Christ is indeed serious, and we should
grasp at once its implications. This is enough to turn a
man's life upside down. Moreover, we have reached a critical
point in the history of the world, where we are aware, in a
confused way, that the charity of the Lord, if it is not to be
unfulfilled, if it is not to be a dead letter, must expand,
grow, be put into practice, within dimensions going beyond
anything in the past. We do not know how to love. I do not
say that we do not want to love. I do not say that we have
not a genuine desire to love. I do not say that we do not love
in our hearts. I say that this is not enough. We still have to
learn how to love in practice.

Moreover, since it is on this that we shall be judged,
that the world will be judged; since there is no religion
without love, since we cannot love God if we do not carry
out the demands of charity to the furthest limit, we must, in
consequence, become aware of the obligations which weigh
upon us in this field. Besides, men look to the Church: they
see how Christians live, and expect from them some such
manifestation of love. Perhaps they have not found it. We
have then, a duty, whatever goodwill and good intentions
we may have, to search our hearts and ask why men do not
find in Christianity this sign of love.

We must reflect deeply, and enter into this mystery of
the heart of Christ, which places us at the centre of humanity – at this point of union between the mystery of the Holy

Trinity, source of life eternal, and our life here on earth. Having done so, we must resolve to learn to give expression in our lives (in accordance with how we are placed) to this supreme mystery of the love of Christ and of men.

6 Loving our Brothers with Jesus
(continued)

When we are confronted on the one hand with the demands of divine charity, the charity of the heart of Christ and on the other with the plight of human beings – their needs and what they are entitled to expect one from another – we cannot help feeling some dismay.

It is impossible to give to God what we ought to give him without being led to reflect on all that should be changed in our own lives, so that we may be able to look the Lord in the face, in peace of mind. It is with misgivings and in a spirit of humility that I would like to put before you the following thoughts. They may cause us pain, but they should also bring us peace, for (and this is something we should never forget) it is God who created man, God who created us. When we begin to realize with dismay the immensity of the demands made upon man in all his dignity, as Jesus intends him to be, we should at the same time re-main fully aware of our weakness and our limitations, accepting these for what they are, without being dis-couraged – remembering that God knows well of what clay we are made.

If we think it is enough to love men in the sanctuary of our hearts – to be full of good wishes and intentions, doing for them, as we say, 'our little best' – then we fail com-pletely to understand the words of the Lord: 'By this all men will know that you are my disciples, if you love one another.' For it would have no sense. Our love must corre-

spond to truth. It must be visible to all. It must draw men.
It must respond to their expectations and give them hope,
so that this love is, for them, a sign that reveals Christ.
For a sign must be something visible, something which
attracts attention. To love discreetly in our hearts, is not
enough: good intentions are not enough. If, moreover, we
look at mankind, we are compelled to admit all the evil
men do, all the sufferings they inflict on one another, all
the unhappiness they heap upon humanity. Yet, if we could
see into their hearts, read their thoughts, we would be
surprised to discover that almost all, certainly the vast
majority, have goodwill: they want to love; they believe
that they love when, in fact, they are doing wrong – and
sometimes even in the name of love, in the name of the
common good, in the name of an ideal. Man, in a word,
does not know how to love. And so we realize the impos-
sibility of separating the will from the intelligence, the heart
from the mind, love from the knowledge of what is the
true good of men. Love can wither. Love can be lacking
in vision – because it is to some extent blind. Numerous
children are unhappy: they are in a state of revolt against
life, because their parents have loved them inadequately.
Yet if we were to see into the heart of a mother of such
children we would find a poor bewildered woman who has
lost her bearings and is quite unable to understand why,
for example, her son is unhappy: she does not know, and
she has not known, how to love. And if the heads of states
do harm to their country, and we looked into their hearts,
we would find very often that these men, again, are well-
wishing, that they lack insight rather than love. Most
ideologies spring from a disinterested desire for the well-
being of mankind. When Karl Marx, in his attic, deeply
resenting the appalling conditions of the worker, began to
write his book which was to have considerable repercussions, to the detriment of many, he was committing an error:
he was unaware of this – it was understanding he lacked,

D

not love, for he loved generously. And we could continue for a long time this enquiry into the hidden recesses of the human heart.

And so we have good reason to question ourselves as to what we should do, if we are to love in truth. What does charity, in the concrete sense, mean in our lives? Is it generosity? Forgetfulness of self? Friendly feelings towards others? Is it devotion to the service of our fellow men? No. All that is without doubt necessary, and is part of charity, but that is not enough. There is no human perfection without truth. Truth. Charity means loving as God loves, because it is a love that is measured by the truth of God, the truth as to man's final end, the truth as to man redeemed by Christ. That is why charity is not easy and why there is no true charity without true faith. Granted there can be charity in the hearts of those who do not know Christ. But this charity is incomplete, and its reality presupposes at least a glimmering of truth, or else that its orientation, under the impulse of grace, transcends a purely human ideal.

In the past things were quite different. It was enough to give alms, to make gifts to the poor in the neighbourhood. Or we could offer our services to the sick in the hospital in our district. We could try to do good within the framework of the society to which we belonged. Yet, of the rest of the world beyond our city or country, we knew nothing. Charity was simple to put into practice, when the role of the intelligence was more limited and an unselfish nature, coupled with common-sense, was often enough.

On this subject we must, I think, examine ourselves. There is the question put by one of those who came to Christ asking: 'Who is my neighbour?' The Lord answered with the parable of the good Samaritan. A Jew was injured and left at the roadside. Those who passed by were Jews and they did not stop, for all sorts of reasons which they probably thought justifiable. It was a Samaritan who came to the rescue. We would do well, at this point, to recall another episode related in the Gospel. Jesus was seated by the well of Jacob, when a woman of Samaria came to draw water. 'Give me some water to drink,' Jesus said to her. 'What? Do you, who are a Jew, ask a woman of Samaria to give you water to drink? Do you not know that there is nothing in common between us?' Minor tribal divisions, religious divisions, national divisions, made a gulf between two peoples separated by a few kilometres! Jesus, when he wanted to give a lesson in the universal quality of love, took the example which could be best understood by the Jews and Samaritans of his times. And so a principle has been established. A frontier has been crossed. Love has no frontiers.

Who then, is our neighbour? This is a question which inevitably presents itself. For if the quality of our charity, if its depth, if, too, the disinterestedness of our motives can grow within our hearts and find expression in prayer, it is not the same when it comes to putting charity into practice when so many persons are involved. To do this, we must know to whom, in particular, we should show our charity. We are only human beings, subject to the limitations of such. And this is what the word neighbour means: a human being – human beings who are near us.

I was saying that in the past the idea of neighbour was relatively easy to define. Today this idea is turned upside down, so that Christians are, one might say, outstripped in the practice of charity and no longer know what to do. For many the idea of charity remains too narrow. They do not think: they are content to practice charity in relation to family, neighbours, and the poor they happen to encounter. There have been, also, charitable appeals made in church – causes presented to the faithful as deserving of support. And so we find little by little that our consciences are troubled, because our duty assumes world-wide proportions. We feel uneasy because we do not know how to put into practice this precept of universal love. Who is my neighbour? Can it really be everyone?

A possible reply to this question is, I think: Our neighbour is every human being who is entitled to expect something from us – every human being, I repeat, who is entitled to expect something from us, even if he is far away and we do not know him. Thus, an inhabitant of an under-developed country, who is dying of hunger – or is in want – is entitled to expect that each citizen of a rich country should be aware of his obligations as a citizen and be ready to put these into practice. This is only one example.

We have to admit that in our times there is a risk of Christians no longer knowing how to carry out the commandment of the Lord. And since it all seems beyond them, they are content to adopt a some what passive attitude. We are indeed distressed by the miseries on every side, but what can we do? We are becoming, it is true, aware of the bond that unites all mankind. The need for a world-wide solidarity is brought home to us every day by the news: it makes itself felt in every household, on the television screen and in the press. We are indeed saddened. But, though we feel concern, we also feel powerless. There is, too, the risk of getting used to things; for feelings, in the long run, become blunted. Then, there is a further point. In the world as it is today, even when we want to put love into practice and fulfill the demands of justice and charity, the individual, alone, is powerless. Only groups, countries, international organizations are really in a position to achieve anything. We find, too, that the solution to these problems calls for competence, qualifications, specialized training, as well as the complexities of community services. We are in duty bound to face this fact, when we ask ourselves what is required of us at the level of our personal responsibilities and our particular circumstances. It is perhaps here that charity on the christian level has not yet the scope one would wish, nor has it achieved the results it

should. There are still many Christians who had not sufficiently realized to what extent the carrying out of our
duties to the state and to society has become a demand
of charity – one which formerly found expression, more
directly, through feelings of pity, compassion, and sympathy. In those days, you saw the invalid whom you were
looking after, the poor man who held out his hand to you.
While engaged in an act of charity, you were directly
aware of what was asked of you, and so you were conscious
of the affection, the tenderness, and the respect to which
these recipients of charity were entitled.

Things have changed, and we can do nothing about it.
Nor ought we to regret this. But we should realize the mental effort that we must all make, and the clear thinking that
is required in assessing our duties, if we are to learn how to
love our fellow men. Otherwise no amount of goodwill can
make up for this, nor shall we be able to give expression to
our love. A desire for results is part of the law of love, for the
aim of love is to achieve the good of those whom we love.
The application of charity required considerable infor-
mation and an effort involving thought and planning on a
scale far greater than in the past. This is demanding, and
makes little appeal to the heart and the feelings.

*

Now we come to a further consideration. If love means
procuring the good of man, we must ask then, what, in fact,
is this good. As Christians we know, in the light of Christ,
that we have the complete answer to this question. We
know, by faith, the nature of man's supernatural destiny.
We know what he will become one day. We believe in the
Resurrection. We believe in life everlasting and in salvation
through Jesus Christ. We believe in all these realities towards which man is moving and which give its significance
to history. But meanwhile? What will prove to be the
true good, the immediate good of man here on earth?

Charity requires of us that we discover what is the greatest good for man at the preent time. Once again, we are bound to come up against the limitations of our intelligence. I do not think that in any other sphere are we able to see so forcibly – in so dramatic a manner – our human limitations. I have said that, in the name of love, human beings are made to suffer. Not even those dedicated to spreading the Gospel – including priests, missionaries, as well as men and women living the religious life – are blameless in this respect. Perhaps the conviction that we possess the truth makes us presumptuous sometimes and hinders us from realizing how narrow are certain of our views on what is for the good of man. Even in the perspective of life everlasting, even in the light of the most intense faith, it is not easy to determine what is man's immediate good. This particularly concerns us, and I confess that whenever I face the problem in an attempt to ask myself what people should do in this mater, what missionaries should do in proclaiming the Gospel, I have difficulty in finding an answer. It is, then, with humility and not any facile assurance that we must approach this problem. Faith gives us certainty in all that concerns revealed truth, but the concrete good, the greatest good for men in this or that situation is something we have to find out for ourselves, even if faith can help us. When we recollect ourselves in the presence of the Lord, we ought to be capable of acknowledging that our charity is far from finding the expression it should and that we must use our intelligence unremittingly to enable us to put the truth into practice more effectively.

I would like at this point to give an example of what I mean. It concerns the way in which certain missionaries visualized the preaching of the Gospel to a primitive Indian tribe. One idea of preaching the Gospel rested on the supposition that, since the greatest good for man was life everlasting, the greatest good that can be bestowed on him

here on earth was baptism, the sacraments, and the teaching of the Church. Hence, an abstract, supernaturalistic
vision of man's good. Children were taken more or less by
force from their village, herded together in schools, where at
night the doors had to be locked, because these unfortunate
Indians, craving freedom, tried to escape. There, they were
given instruction, baptized, made to receive the sacraments – and so, it was believed, given the greatest possible
good. Marriages were contracted between young men and
women who had been baptized, and the couples were
settled in artificial villages. This resulted in the creation of a
completely unbalanced society, in which there lived, rather
like beggars around the mission, children robbed of the
happiness of family life, and adults taken out of their milieu
and deprived of the work which they shared in common.
Yet these missionaries were generous-minded priests,
wholly dedicated to the Lord Jesus Christ, their hearts on
fire with charity. But could we possibly say that they understood the greatest good for these Indians? Clearly they were
deceived. I give this instance because it is one of the most
striking examples I know, and one which best enables us
to see to what lengths such errors of judgment can lead. It
is easy to imagine the scandal this must have caused, and
the reactions of competent lay persons – those who realize
how necessary to the true development of man, and hence
to his greatest good, is a well balanced community, along
with the human and social qualities that it engenders.

It is indeed difficult to 'situate' human life, short as it is,
in the face of life eternal: it is difficult to define satisfac-
torily what is the greatest good here on earth. To attempt
to do so is already difficult for those who have in view the
good of the temporal city. It is much more difficut to
define this in the perspective of life eternal and the spreading
of the Gospel.

True, the problem will not always present itself in a
form so acute. But we will always be under an obligation

to determine the good which charity ought to procure, in relation to the condition of the world as it is. This question is asked by all men of goodwill. We should, therefore, put ourselves in the presence of the Lord, and ask what it is he requires of us. Let us not over-simplify the problem. For, in an effort to find an answer, man's intelligence has to incur today the considerable risk of being crushed – controlled by organizations that it has itself brought into being and which it cannot do without. Now, there is the same danger in the Church, which is also under an obligation to make use of the intelligence when availing itself of apostolic organisations more complex than in the past.

We have to approach our epoch with great humility and, at the same time, with great hope in our hearts. With great humility, because we are obliged to accept imperfections, slowness in achievement, errors which cause us suffering – and this even in the functioning of the Church. We should accept humbly and realistically our human condition along with its defects. The church implanted in pagan society the leaven of charity and of freedom. Even so, a long time passed before slavery was suppressed. The Church has sometimes been reproached for this slowness: sufficient account has not been taken of the situation as it then was and the inadequate means of social action at the Church's disposal. The Church started, indeed, a spiritual ferment, but it needed time for this to change men's hearts. It would however, be too easy a solution, and a false one, if we were to use slowness in the past as an excuse in our own era to assume everything will settle itself, without an effort being made. We must analyse how things are and reflect that they are no longer as they used to be. Today, evolution, both of the individual and of society, is not only rapid and far reaching, it is a process of which man is fully conscious and which he intends to control: it is not, as formerly, a passive transformation whereby society and the individual were left to take their course. Society has assumed a new character. This entails enormous risks, but it is also a challenge to man's greatness. This newly won responsibility demands from him a proportionately greater magnanimity and charity. Purity of heart and a true vision of man, revealed by the light of faith, must illumine the intellect and thus dispose it to understand better what is for the good of humanity.

*

Having considered briefly, on the one hand, the heart of the Lord and what he expects from us, and, on the other, the situation in which man finds himself today, we should not allow ourselves to feel disquietude. We must, rather, be in readiness to take action, while remaining at the same time at peace and always open to reality, so as to resolve better the problems that confront us. This is a matter which concerns the personal lives of all of us here and our responsibility in guiding Christians.

If there is a view of spirituality which is false, it is the one which presents it as a kind of interior life lived in the abstract, in pursuit of an intellectual ideal, without reference to things as they really are. That is why the expression 'interior life' is not without danger, if it encourages us to confine our religion and our relations with God to within ourselves – without reflecting sufficiently that this interior life, if it is truly lived with God, must completely change our way of living and our attitude regarding our duties to others and our own ministry. While maintaining peace of mind, we should have a healthy restiveness, which will prevent us from coming to a standstill in our evolution. The whole man is redeemed, and through charity, the whole man is involved in relationships with the rest of humanity which should be directed towards the building up of a solidarity, one with another. Nothing eludes the charity of Christ and here, especially, is the supreme task of working for Christian perfection, because we shall be judged on love.

7 Hope in the Compassion of Jesus

The compassion of God, along with his holiness, is perhaps one of the attributes of his divinity that we find most difficult to understand. For it is difficult to know God. We try to do so, beginning with the experience of the sole living and intelligent being whom we know: man. There is, indeed, in the human heart – above all, in the heart of those who are near to God and have been influenced by the Holy Spirit – a kind of mirror reflecting the perfect qualities that belong only to God. But even when we have pondered a whole life time, we do not succeed in knowing God, and when we try to say what he is, or, what is more important, to make our lives conform with what we think God is, we are always aware of our limitations. We are disconcerted by the opposition that must, it seems, exist between the rigour of God's holiness – the holiness of the Holy One, of the thrice Holy – and his compassion. How can one approach God without being spotless, and how can his compassion fail to cast a shadow on his holiness? Such is the dilemma posed by a God who is infinitely holy and infinite in compassion.

Our hearts must become like that of our Lord, since we are called to be perfect as God, our Father, is perfect. And when we look at ourselves and think about the judgment of God, we are gripped with fear. What does it mean to see the face of God? What is required of us if we are to be able to see God? Purgatory is not some kind of artificial, arbitrary purification: it is the final transformation of love, so that we may be purified to the extent of being able to endure the gaze of God. We cannot look God in the face without there being a complete purity in the love that we give to him. The compassion of God is not deceived, and, God being Love and Truth, his compassion is itself Truth. It is the Truth of the look of the Creator directed upon the being he has made. Only his Creator can know the heart of man, the weakness of man, the goodwill of man. Only the heart of the Saviour can know the way we must follow if we are to be purified in the blood of Christ. And we should think of this purification not as a kind of juridical pardon, but a transformation which really assimilates us, in truth, to Christ, and so enables us to see God and be united to him for ever.

Already in the Old Testament the compassion of God is made manifest. We should read in the Prophets, one after the other, the continual interchange between Israel, the sinner and the rebel, and her Lord who has chosen her. There are imprecations expressing God's anger, and reconciliations without end, which might suggest weakness on the part of God: there are expressions of tenderness as of a mother, or a shepherd in search of sheep that have gone astray; we have here only pale reflections of a compassion which is not weakness. In us, such an attitude could, perhaps, be weakness: in God it is an attribute proper to his divine nature. That is why we cannot replace the word 'compassion' by any other. It is not pity. It is not simply pardon. It is something else. Only God can be compassionate: if we are compassionate it is to the extent that we resemble God – to the extent that our hearts are enlightened by the Holy Spirit – and perhaps it is through a kind of 'melting' of the heart, experienced by some of the saints, that we can begin to understand the nature of compassion.

We know the norms of holiness, first through the Law and the Prophets; then through the commandments and counsels of Christ. Now, the Lord himself teaches us that the precept of love, this two-fold precept, is the foundation of the Law and the Prophets. By ourselves we can, if we think about it, understand that, if the moral precepts have this foundation, they are not arbitrary; but we are not able, by the sole light of reason, to understand this foundation to the extent of being able to deduce all the demands of the moral law. God is himself the ultimate foundation to the extent of being able to deduce all the demands of the moral law. God is himself the ultimate foundation, for he is life itself, and so the measure and the perfection of all life. It is only in him and through him that we can get to know all the laws applicable to human life: our lives in accordance with the spirit, our lives as children of God. God is the source of all life. That is why he does not judge as we judge. It is, then, above all in the heart of Christ that we shall discover the meaning of compassion.

Jesus knew what was in the heart of man. As the Gospel tells us: 'He had no need to be taught by anyone: he knew what was in man.' We may be tempted to conclude that Jesus, just because he had this knowledge, would surely have looked down on man – lost confidence in him. But Jesus took a different attitude. He was, in fact, sent through the compassion of God; that is why he came to save, 'not to judge'. He says this more than once. He shocked his contemporaries, because he was no respecter of persons, whereas our immediate reaction is to judge others, put them in categories. There are the Pharisees, there are the tax collectors, there are the sinners, the women of the streets. There are the righteous; there are those who think them-selves righteous. There are the heathen, the Jews, the Greeks. We never cease judging people by their behaviour, their appearance – measuring them by what we regard as the canon or ideal of what is right. Jesus broke down these categories and scandalized the righteous or those who be-lieved themselves such. He ate with the tax collectors and sinners and drank wine with them. He made it clear that he was drawn to the poor and the despised, just because they were put into that category. Sitting before the Temple and watching the faithful, who, as they went in, dropped a coin into the alms box, he could not help exclaiming in admiration: no one had noticed that a woman, who was poor, had put into the box the one small coin she had. 'The others gave of their abundance,' Jesus said, 'she gave all.' The Lord reads our hearts. And the poor Canaanite woman, obscure and humble, knowning herself one of the heathen, knowing herself rejected by Israel, the chosen people, spoke the language of the poor in heart: 'The little dogs are content with the crumbs thrown from their master's table.' Jesus seemed to contradict her, because he wanted to draw attention to the greatness of the woman's faith: 'In truth I have not found in Israel such faith as in this woman.' When Jesus described the feast given by the rich man, while Lazarus, the poor man was crouching in front of the door, ignored by all, we realize that the heart of the Lord is with Lazarus. It is Lazarus who will be taken up to Paradise in Abraham's bosom. And when, as he drew near to a town, Jesus was surrounded by cheering crowds who tried to see him close at hand, he left them and went to call Zacchaeus, who was sitting up in his sycamore tree – he was very short and wanted to see Jesus. Now, Zacchaeus, it was known, had extorted money while acting in his official capacity. Even so, Jesus said to him: 'Zacchaeus, come down quickly for I must spend today at your home.' What Jesus did scandalized the whole town. He also scandalized the Pharisee who had invited him, because he let a woman of the streets come near to him. 'If this man were a prophet, he would know who this woman is, what sort of person: a public sinner.' And this sinner touched Jesus and he let her do so. 'Simon, I have something to say to you.' And Jesus, after he had contrasted the attitude of the woman with that of the Pharisee, went on: 'Because she loved much, much will be forgiven her. Whoever is forgiven little, loves little.' Words full of mystery. When Jesus held a long conversation with a woman of Samaria, near the well of Jacob, the Apostles were astonished, almost scandalized. How was it that the Lord was talking so intimately with a woman and, what is more, a woman of Samaria known to be living an irregular life – she had already had several husbands and the man with whom she was now living was not her husband? Nevertheless Jesus took her into his confidence: he went to the length even of revealing to her that he was the Messiah. There is also the woman taken in adultery: 'Let him who is without sin throw the first stone,' and he went on: 'Neither do I condemn you. Go, and sin no more.'

Jesus forgave, but he did not forgive gratuitiously. He forgave because he found humility of heart, because he found an attitude of truth, the truth which is deep within a person beyond outward appearances. And, in agony on the cross, when he took upon himself the burden of the whole world, Jesus found time to turn to the thief at his side, of whom no one was taking any notice, for, after all, this man was justly condemned. It was to him Jesus gave his entire attention during his last moments, saying that he would take him with him: 'In truth, I tell you, today you will be with me in paradise.'

This aspect of the heart of Christ is the one that we have perhaps the greatest difficulty in understanding, although we may think we understand. Yes, we believe we understand. In reality, it is here, specially, we are in need of enlightenment – for this, more than any other, is the divine aspect of Christ by which he reveals most deeply his knowledge both of God and the heart of man. 'They know not what they do,' he says when praying to his Father to forgive those who are torturing him before he is put to death. 'They know not what they do.' That is why they are to be forgiven. Do we know what we do when, in our relations with God, we sin? We do not know. And it is because God knows, it is because Jesus knows, that he is compassionate – because he who knows all is looking upon one who does not know. We understand, then, what Jesus felt for the multitudes; for all those unfortunate persons who, in his eyes, are as sheep, 'abandoned because they have no shepherd'. He meant by this that they are without anyone who is to lead them on the path to God. Left to themselves, how could they know?

Here we are confronted with the mystery of man. Why has God made this creature, man, so feeble, so ignorant? Why is there sin? Why is it difficult to know God? On this point, as on the problem of evil, the Lord has explained nothing. How could he explain? But we have God's answer in the revelation of his compassion. In this way God revealed that he knew what he was doing when he created man, and, because he knew, he himself had to show the way to man and treat him for what he is, as a Father treats his little son. There is no unjustice on the part of God in treating man as a child, since that is what, in fact, he is in the sight of God and will always remain so.

'You who are heavily laden, come to me and I will give you rest. I am gentle and humble of heart,' says the Lord. 'He will not break the bruised reed nor quench the smoking flax.' And that is how it is with us. We are never completely broken, but we are indeed bowed down and bruised: and if our inner fire does not burn with a bright flame, the hearth still smokes. That is why we must go to the Lord in confidence. He is the God of life; he is not the God of death. He wants life. He wants the sinner to live, not die. Most of the miracles performed by the Lord are in the nature of signs of his hidden action in our souls: the blind see, the lame walk, those who are bowed down are made upright; the deaf hear, and, he adds, the poor have the gospel preached to them. We have here human poverty in all its forms. And Jesus had come, above all else, to heal that poverty. This, surely, is what he meant in pronouncing these words in reply to messengers sent by John the Baptist (then in prison) to ask Jesus: 'Are you really the Messiah?' For in spite of his faith and his holiness, John the Baptist, it seems, had been somewhat taken off his guard by the humility shown by Christ and the absence of startling Messianic signs of the kind expected by Israel. And the response made by Jesus was as we have said.

At Nazareth – the town where Jesus had been brought up, where he had passed so many years sharing, unnoticed, the common lot of family and social life – his townspeople had great difficulty in believing in him, because they knew him too well: they had seen him close at hand without finding in him anything that was not simple, genuine, ordinary. In the synagogue he took the scroll of the law and began to read the passage from Isasiah: 'The Spirit of the Lord is upon me, because he has anointed me; he has sent me to bring the good news to the poor, to proclaim liberty to the captives, to restore sight to the blind, bring freedom to those in captivity.' But they could not believe in him when he said afterwards: 'He it is whom you see now.'

There is yet another wonderful thing: the joy of God and heaven when one sinner repents. We are not told there is the same degree of joy over a righteous man who has not fallen away. Consider the parable of the prodigal son. The father gets up, takes the initiative, runs to meet his son, falls on his neck, embraces him, while the son is busy thinking how best to approach his father, how to justify himself, win pardon. But the father does not wait: he does not give his son time to make excuses. Quite the contrary: they must kill the fatted calf, hold a feast, enjoy themselves. It was this which scandalized the son who had remained dutiful. Now, we are often dutiful sons (or we think we are), in that, without admitting it, we count ourselves among those who behave well in the sight of men – among worthy, respectable persons. And we must not forget, either, the joy felt by the shepherd who found the lost sheep; nor that of the woman who found, at last, the coin she had lost.

We should pray to God to make us understand the secret of his compassion and the truth it implies. We need this light first of all for ourselves, as the foundation of our hope. To the joy of God and heaven at the return of the sinner who repents, there should correspond our joy (the joy, that is, of those who repent and run to the Lord) at being the cause of joy to God. We may presume to say: Happy the man who sins if, in so doing, he learns humility and realizes a little better the truth of how he stands in the sight of God. We are weary of repeating the same things in confession; we are weary of what we feel to be our stagnation, our mediocrity; we are weary of living within our limitations, of discovering that we are not saints. But perhaps we have difficulty in realizing the truth because our conception of sanctity is possibly not entirely correct. We ought to live in the joy of hope, in the certainty of being loved and saved – in short, in the acceptance of the truth.

Thérèse of the Child Jesus used to say that, even if she had committed the greatest crimes on earth, she would be sure of God's forgiveness. She went on to say that, in the presence of God, it is best to be very small, for if one is small all is forgiven, and if one falls it is not from a great height. There we have an important secret of hope: a solid and lofty view of faith, not mere sentimentality. For there is no question of misrepresenting the compassion of God, which is not weakness, nor is it simply kindness or pity: it is something different. It is the vision of the Creator looking upon his work; the vision of the Saviour looking on his work of redemption, on his creature whom he has redeemed.

When we confess our sins, we should tell ourselves that we are going to meet the heart of a compassionate God, to find, there, joy and consolation. We should not dwell too much on ourselves. It will not help to look at ourselves too closely. That is not going to enable us to advance on the way of perfection. At the beginning of the spiritual journey there is hard work to be done within ourselves, which de-

E

pends on the resoluteness with which we use our will and on the strength of our resolutions; determination, but the more we go forward on the path to God, the more we shall learn by experience that we reach a point beyond which we know we can attain nothing. There even comes a moment when we seem to have done all we can. And yet we must continue on our way, continue to grow, continue to draw closer to God, for we must never come to a standstill. There is, then, a time in the spiritual life when we cannot do otherwise than become contemplatives, if we have to draw nearer to God. There is a kind of refining of our hearts and our minds: a perfecting of our actions, which only the Spirit of God can bring about, making us, to some degree, like the Lord.

Peter sinned in denying his Master. But Jesus knew him. He knew well that, in this case, the sin was not really deliberate. Yet such a lapse was formally, objectively grave. We would probably have judged Peter very severely. How could he have betrayed his Master three times over? We would have reproached him with cowardice and treachery. Three times, one after another, he was afraid, in front of a servant girl, of being judged unfavourably: he was afraid of being judged by men. But the Lord knew the heart of him whom he had himself chosen. Men would have condemned Peter, we would have condemned him; for the Lord, it sufficed to look at him. 'He looked at him.' We can imagine all that there must have been in this look of the Lord, for Peter burst into sobs, regained his confidence, became more anxious than ever to serve his Master, more faithful than ever. Judas also repented. It is said in the Scriptures that he repented – that is to say, he realized the wrong he had done, the magnitude of the fault he had committed, but he did not cease from looking at himself; he did not look at the Lord; he was not able to meet his look. But we can be certain that, if he had met the look of the Lord, he would not have hanged himself in despair.

And so we should find comfort, joy and, above all, perhaps, this desire, this possibility of continuing to grow in the love of the Lord in confidence, thus learning to enter into the compassionate love of Jesus.

8   Hope in the Compassion of Jesus
   (continued)

'Be compassionate as your Father is compassionate,' the
Lord has said to us. We must read again the parable of the
servant whose debt his master had cancelled, when he
deserves to go to prison. On leaving his master's house, immediately after the debt has been remitted, he meets one
of his comrades who owes him a small sum. And what does
he do? He claims his rights, and drags the other into prison
until he has payed what he owes to the last farthing.
You know the master's stern reaction: 'Should you not
have pardoned him, even as I have cancelled your debt.'
'Forgive us our faults as we forgive,' the Lord makes us say
in the prayer that he has taught us. 'As we forgive those who
have offended us.' Neither more nor less. And the Lord adds:
'In the measure that you measure, it will be measured to
you.' 'With the judgment you judge, you will be judged.'
When we reflect upon this, have we not, here, one of the
most formidable sayings of Christ, if we think, in honesty,
of the casual way in which we judge others?

I have just spoken about compassion. On the day of
judgment will not the Lord find that we have judged our
brothers too hastily, without sufficient awareness of our
responsibilities? If we want to be perfect, if we claim to
belong to the Lord, we must take seriously all he tells us
on this matter.

We must first of all learn to forgive. You know the question that Peter put to Jesus: 'Lord, how many times should

I forgive the wrongs my brother has committed against me? As often as seven times?' Peter was referring, no doubt, to someone who committed the same fault over and over again – an habitual offender. 'I say to you not seven times, but seventy times seven,' his Master answered – which means that there is no limit to the number of times we should forgive.

But what does it mean to forgive? Is a mere word enough, spoken a little condescendingly, showing that we will not persist in our displeasure, that we will behave on the surface as if nothing had happened? This is not enough; we have to be able to speak from the heart.

Compassion goes much deeper. When the Lord asks us not to judge, he is thinking of our hearts, of an inner attitude of complete truth. It is impossible to separate in man the interior from the exterior. 'The mouth speaks out of the abundance of the heart.' And if our hearts are not true, if they are not just, if they are not filled with gentleness and respect for others, if we do not refrain, in all sincerity, from passing judgment, we can no longer refrain from sinning in word. Are we as aware as we should be of the grave wounds inflicted by the spreading of rumours, by judgments lightly passed? These are the wounds that are difficult to heal. It is not a bad thing to meditate sometimes on this stinging text in which Saint James speaks to us about the tongue: 'He who makes no error in what he says is a perfect man.' Moreover, he compares our tongue to the rudder of a ship. 'However large they are, ships, when lashed by violent winds, are steered by a very small rudder, at the will of the pilot. In the same way the tongue is very small, yet it can boast about great matters.' Our tongue governs almost everything in our lives and Saint James draws a comparison between the wild animals which man has succeeded in taming and his tongue, which, small though it is, he has not tamed. And if man cannot control his tongue, then he is not yet able to control his heart. It is impossible to separate the lips from the heart, so strong is the unity in man. The more open we are, the more true to ourselves' the more will the tongue reflect the heart, as does our way of looking at someone, our entire attitude, or the kind of welcome we give. Everything betrays the inner self. An attitude of mind, a feeling of superiority, of which we are scarcely aware, can reveal itself in our manner.

In short, we should not pass judgment in our hearts. Above all we should not judge someone's intentions simply from appearance. But are we not sometimes obliged to pass judgment? We must learn to know others, and then pass on them some degree of judgment – if only to enable us to give advice to a person who asks for it? Yes, we must learn to know our brothers: we do not know them well enough. We can live beside someone for years without really getting to know him. It is astonishing to find, even in an apparently united home, that man and wife, after years of life together do not know each other in any depth. And I say nothing of religious communities.

There is taking place today, for better or for worse, a scientific advance in the investigation into man's consciousness, in the study of the unconscious, in the knowledge of complexes, and in all the psychological phenomena which impede or diminish man's freedom and are conducive to deterministic attitudes. Whatever is true in this field can, and should, be assimilated into a spiritual and supernatural vision of man, and this can teach us to judge our brothers in the light, first, of truth, and, then, of compassion. Whereas God knows in a single glance, because he has made us, we learn only little by little, after a slow progress in psychology. Between the view implying that man is at all times perfectly free and totally responsible for his actions, and the opposite view which is disposed to affirm that his actions are all more or less determined, there is a mean which will enable us to comprehend better the weakness of man's will. Yes, we must understand that man is the victim of certain compulsions, yet, at the same time, be convinced that he need never despair of himself. In the sight of God every human being can, and should, hope to be saved. This can be so, for the compassion of God rests upon truth. It is for us to adopt such an attitude in so far as we can – above all when, in the confessional, we should help people not to despair of themselves and not to despair of God's pardon. A human being should never, and can never, be driven to despair. If the Lord has told us that we should forgive without limit, does not that amount to saying that perhaps there are some who cannot always, in spite of good intentions, avoid falling again. We ought to teach such persons not to despair of themselves. We ought to teach them hope.

The Lord tells us not to judge. Now, as we have said, we are sometimes obliged to judge. What Jesus means is that we ought not to judge with intent to condemn. Let us not condemn. We have no right to do this without the risk of being ourselves condemned. We must not judge by appearances. Who knows the heart of man except God? Yet, we spend our time judging by appearances, as if we knew men's hearts. This is something to which we should give thought.

We often hear – from the lips of some of the young, especially when they are talking of how they were received by a community of nuns or priests – the comment that they felt themselves immediately judged. Or, on the contrary, they will say they were at ease because they did not feel judged. 'I don't feel I'm judged.' They mean by this that they do not feel the object of a critical appraisal which at once draws conclusions from a person's manner or attitude, or perhaps a way of speaking. They do not feel they are put into categories, judged in accordance with a set of rules and regulations by which we are inclined to classify people, without troubling to put ourselves in their place.

There is nothing new in this. It is a very old problem. Here again Saint James speaks to us: 'My brothers, you who believe in the Lord Jesus Christ, the Lord of glory, do not treat people in different ways because of their outward appearances. Suppose a rich man wearing a gold ring and grand garments comes into your gathering and, at the same time, a poor man in shabby clothes. If you pay more attention to the well-dressed man and say to him, "Sit here, in the place of honour," but to the poor man: "Stand there, where you are, or sit on the floor by my seat," are you not passing judgment on one another? Are you not setting yourselves up as judges from wrong motives?'

Though we are hardly aware of it, we are always – by force of habit or as a result of social or cultural prejudices – embarking on judgments of this kind. I would like to give you two examples.

The first, I confess, is somewhat personal. However, in speaking of it, I shall not give away any secret. Among the Little Brothers there is one who has a rather strange vocation – something like that of Saint Benedict Joseph Labre. He is a contemplative, but he lives the life of a vagrant. After testing his vocation for some years, we let him have his way, for we believed he was answering a genuine call from God, following an authentic vocation. He used to sleep under bridges and live among the very poor, among drop-outs, and those whom society had rejected. This did not stop him from fulfilling his vocation as a Little Brother or from praying for long stretches of time in churches. He travelled across the world as a pilgrim. He often had to ask to be taken in at a presbytery or a convent. You would not believe how often he was turned away and left at the door. There were other times when he felt judged from head to foot, because he wore shabby sandals, his clothing was poor, and he had not the appearance – the appearance, I say – of a religious. But what is a religious? He felt himself judged, and very often harshly, until people got to know him.

And now the second example. It concerns our reactions

in racial and cultural matters. We are all aware of the violently conflicting ideas in the world as it is today. But are we ourselves wholly blameless? When we meet an African or anyone belonging to a race other than our own, whose cultural milieu is totally different from ours, we react automatically. We are used to thinking of coloured people as constantly occupied with manual tasks of a very humble kind: we have so often seen them working as dockers at ports. Also, quite naturally, we are used to thinking of ourselves as belonging to a civilization of a superior kind. Some of the more intelligent Westerners – and even some of the missionaries, when they want to show that they are kindly disposed to Africans – display an exaggerted friendliness in which one is aware of the condescension of someone who knows he is superior. True, this is done almost unconsciously, as everyone would agree. I remember an African student saying to me: 'When shall we be human beings like the others? When shall we be treated like everyone else? I spend my time meeting people who either look down on me or show their respect by exceptional attentions, so that I'm never able to forget who I am and be accepted just as an ordinary human being.'

The bishop of an African see who wanted to establish Catholic Action in his diocese brought from a district in Paris a chaplain who belonged to the Young Catholic Workers. He was harshly criticized by his missionaries who said to each other: 'How can this task be entrusted to a priest who doesn't know coloured people and has no experience of them? Why – when we know the Africans well – call in a priest from Europe to deal with the Young Catholic Workers here?' In fact this chaplain made immediate contact with the young men and won their confidence, precisely because, forgetting they were black, he treated them as he would have treated workers in Paris.

We must admit that we have not yet succeeded in eradicating totally our feelings of superiority over other races.

No, we have not rid ourselves of such feelings, even if we believe the contrary. We are not yet able to behave towards these others with the complete simplicity and openness due to human beings. We are ostentatious in our friendliness, which only reveals our underlying, unacknowledged, feeling of superiority.

This is a serious matter. When we want to follow our Lord to the end, the transfiguration of our being by grace must reach into our very depths – into the subconscious areas of our being. This needs to be understood. First, so that we may not be discouraged by the reactions in us. Secondly, that we may become more humble, more sincere, and realize that only the Holy Spirit is able to give a total perfection and simplicity to our love which cannot be entirely genuine until the deepest areas of our being – where these reactions are rooted – have been purified. To such an extent has original sin left its mark upon us.

The perfecting of our charity is the work of the Holy Spirit. We must ask that this be granted to us. We must have the humility to hear the Holy Spirit, and the intelligence to make possible the action of the Spirit within us.

9 Witnesses to the Resurrection of Jesus

'If Christ is not risen, our teaching is vain,' Saint Paul wrote, 'our faith, too, is vain. And so we are false witnesses.' And when, to replace the Apostle who had betrayed Jesus, the Eleven decided to choose another, they thought it essential for the apostolate that this man should be one of those who had witnessed the life and the Resurrection of the Lord.

Having accompanied the Apostles while they followed the Lord, we will now accompany them as they learn to believe in the Resurrection of their Master.

We know that for Jesus himself this sign of his Resurrection was unique. 'This generation demands a sign, and for a sign it will be given that of the prophet Jonas.' It is hard to know with any certainty what the Apostles thought about the Lord, when they began to believe in him as the Messiah. We know that in the Jewish world many traditions pointed to the glorious figure of the Messiah, and we can assume that when Jesus began to manifest his power by his first miracles, the Apostles must have been disposed to believe that Jesus could not die. The Messiah, as Israel thought of him, was someone outstanding, indeed unique – his kingly aspect had been presented with such majesty and glory that we can understand why the Apostles refused to listen to the predictions, repeated by Jesus, as to his death. They could neither imagine nor understand such a thing. Now the predictions of the Resurrection were associated with those of the Passion. But the idea of the Passion was contrary to all they believed about Jesus: they had preconceived ideas.

However, Jesus revealed himself as Lord of life and of death. He brought back to life the little daughter of Jairus. At Nain he brought back to life the young man, the only son of a widow, who was on the way to his burial. And, as a consequence, the Gospel adds, the renown of Jesus spread far and wide: the fact of restoring life to the dead could not fail to awake astonishment and enthusiasm among the crowds. These miracles must have confirmed the Apostles in their conviction that Jesus could not suffer death, since he was himself Lord of death.

When Jesus took with him his three chosen Apostles to the summit of Mount Tabor he revealed himself to them in such dazzling splendour that there could be no doubt whatever that he was the Messiah. Moreover the Messianic tradition had alluded to the fact that the Messiah would appear between Moses and Elias. Now these same Apostles are the ones who accompanied Jesus to Gethsemane. It is amazing to what lengths Jesus went to conceal his Transfiguration. This radiant sign was witnessed by three persons only, and these were to keep silence until his Resurrection from the dead. We understand, now, what was in the mind of the Lord; he wanted to strengthen the faith of the Apostles, so that the Passion might not scandalize them. In the eastern liturgy the feat of the Transfiguration emphasises this aspect of the revelation on Mount Tabor.

We are coming to one of the most significant moments in the life of Jesus: the resurrection of Lazarus. This man was his friend – so much so that when Jesus learnt of his death he was deeply distressed: he wept, even though he knew he was going to raise Lazarus from the dead. This causes us astonishment. But it is also reassuring, for death remains death: a mystery that is terrifying even in the light of Jesus, even if we are friends of Jesus and know we will be raised from the dead by him. This incident is also a highlight in the life of Jesus, because the Passion is so near: he regards this miracle as having special importance for the faith of his Apostles. He says to them: 'I am glad you were not there, that you may believe.' The resurrection of Lazarus caused a considerable stir at Jerusalem: people came from all over the place to see the man who had been brought back to life. But Jesus is very near the hour of his death. The Last Supper has come, and his parting discourse: 'I shall not leave you orphans, I shall return to you; you will see me because I live and you will live.' At the time the Apostles did not understand these words any more than they understood others, for they did not believe their Master would die. And when Jesus alluded to his Resurrection, saying: 'Destroy this temple and I will build it again in three days,' this saying remained for them a closed book. Nevertheless sadness began to make itself felt among them, for they realized in a confused kind of way that something grave was going to happen. They knew there were those who were looking for their Master, to arrest him. 'You also are sad now, but I shall see you again and your hearts will rejoice and your joy no man will take from you.' The joy promised by Jesus, that none can take from us, is it not the joy of knowing that he is risen from the dead.

The Passion and death of Jesus, his burial, the dispersal of the Apostles – these events come one after another. And we see how often, in the happenings that follow his Resurrection, Jesus goes to every possible lengths to make the Apostles believe he has risen, before they have actually seen him with their own eyes. It is remarkable. First, they see only the empty tomb. True, in the case of the women, there are the angels who try to assure them that the body of Jesus is not there: 'One should not seek the living among the dead.' And the angels go on: 'Remember what he said to you in Galilee: "I shall rise again".' Jesus is not visible – he does not reveal himself yet, but the angels recall the prophetic words of Jesus: one must believe. The Apostles, however, did not believe what the woman told them. Peter and John ran to the tomb. John saw the folded shroud and the rolled napkin. 'He saw and he believed,' the Gospel says. That is to say he remembered, then, the predictions of Jesus. In the heart of John there had been such love for Jesus that this gave him a perceptivity which enabled him to believe that his Master was indeed risen.

Jesus appeared to Cephas, as well as to the disciples on the road to Emmaus. It was only after that, when the Apostles together, that they really believed that Jesus had risen. He appeared to them when they were gathered round the supper table. And as if he guessed all that was passing in their unbelieving hearts, he asked them for something to eat, to show he was not a ghost. 'Why all this perplexity? . . . See my hands and my feet. Touch me and ask yourselves if a spirit has flesh or bones, as you see I have.' And then, when they still did not believe, he said to them: 'Have you something to eat here?' And when Thomas, who had not been with the others, joined them eight days afterwards, Jesus said to him: 'Happy are those who believe without seeing.' Without seeing! This, it appears, was one Beatitude more: 'Happy are those who have believed without seeing.'

Then the appearances of Christ came one after another. This new stage in the lives of the Apostles left them somewhat bewildered, because, though they had the joy of seeing Jesus again, he was no longer with them in the same manner as before: he appeared, then went away. The Apostles give the impression of no longer knowing what they ought to do. The women had told them, on behalf of Jesus, that they should go into Galilee – there they would see him again. We know what took place on the shore of Lake Tiberias: 'It is the Lord.' No one dared question him: they were overawed, yet, they knew that it was Jesus. They shared with him the food that he had himself prepared.

After this there is the Ascension: the final departure of Jesus. What happened is recorded in two sentences: 'He departed from them and was taken up into heaven.' And since then no one has seen Jesus as he was on earth.

The long silence, the departure from the world of him who was the first to conquer death – to die no more – is indeed a mystery. The other instances of persons brought back from the dead by Jesus are totally different: in each case it was a matter of returning to await a second death, whereas Jesus neither dies any more nor is he any longer on earth.

What does our belief in the Resurrection amount to? First, the Resurrection of Jesus, then our own? Saint Paul, who saw Jesus on the road to Damascus but did not live in his company or witness his death and Resurrection, as had the other Apostles, writes: 'I have handed on to you that which I myself received concerning the death of the Lord, his burial, and his Resurrection.' And he listed those who had witnessed the appearances of the living Christ: 'He appeared to Cephas, then to the Twelve. After that he appeared to more than five hundred brethren at once – the greater number of them are still living. Then he appeared to James; then, to all the Apostles.' We feel that Saint Paul is very near to this happening. Moreover we can imagine those hours and days between the Passion and the Ascension – what they must have meant to the Apostles; the impact they must have made upon their memories and their hearts. The Apostles bore no witness to this until Pentecost. But already they felt a joy which no one could take from them. The Ascension took them a little off their guard. This time, they thought, all was ended. They would see Jesus no more here on earth. And then there were the words of the angel: 'Why do you stay thus looking up into heaven? He who has been taken away from you, this same Jesus will come in like manner as you have seen him go up into heaven.' Jesus will come. When? Now, to those who had just lived through these events it seemed natural that the time of waiting would not be long. When someone has gone away, a little while ago, saying: 'I shall return,' we expect him to do so quite soon. And in proportion as the centuries pass since the departure of Jesus, the time of his return seems correspondingly more and more remote. We no longer really await this return of Jesus on earth: perhaps we believe in it, but we do not await it.

The foundation of the Apostles' preaching is belief in the Resurrection of Christ. It is a living faith. We proclaim our belief in the Resurrection when we recite the creed. But is it a living faith? And I mean by a living faith one which makes an impact upon our lives today, hour by hour: as a belief in a happening in the reality of which we truly believe. As to our own resurrection, do we await it, believe in it as something which will really take place? The religious life, the consecrated life, the life of chastity only assume their full significance in the perspective of our resurrection that is yet to come. But in the context of the world today it seems beyond the bounds of probability that heaven is a reality. Perhaps we underestimate the difficulties our contemporaries experience in believing in the 'last things'. As to these difficulties, there are factors which we should take into account both to strengthen our own faith and to be able to communicate it to others: for it is our duty to present these divine realities in such a way that they appear as having, at least, probability. If Jesus is living, if he is risen from the dead, if he really cares about men why does he not reveal himself? And if it is true that souls after death enter into another life, how is it that there can be no communication with them? Does not this silence point to the fact that there is nothing? True, some say that the dead have appeared. But these are isolated instances that we cannot present in a scientific or definitive manner. They do not put an end to this mystery as to the silence of the hereafter: this complete, opaque silence. Only our faith can penetrate this silence.

There is also the difficulty of visualizing such things. How are we to speak of the return of Jesus? How will this take place? And the resurrection of the dead? When we think of the multitude of those who will rise from the dead, it is inconceivable: we cannot imagine that all these persons will rise. How many of them will there be? This defies calculation. Furthermore, what, we ask, will all these persons do? Our contemporaries are not disposed to believe in realities which do not attract them, which do not appear to them as desirable. Clearly, to live for ever would in itself be desirable only on condition that such a life were worth living. But how can we make desirable to men of today a world and a life which are stripped of all which makes our present life of interest: the joy of discovery, movement, all that we mean by being alive; advance in knowledge, travel, the exploration of the world. This is what we mean by 'life'. An immobile world going on for ever has no attraction. And the various ways in which heaven was presented during the Middle Ages are of no help. If the paintings of Fra Angelico delight us, we must also admit that they do not· give a picture of heaven that, in our eyes, is either within the bounds of probability or attractive. What shall we do in a haven of this kind? We speak of singing the praises of God. But people cannot imagine what this means. And the Beatific Vision? This is an abstraction. It must, then, be agreed that for the vast majority of Christians heaven is not desirable, because we do not know what it is and we are unable to imagine that it could be interesting or a source of happiness. The plain fact remains that, for men, death is the end of life – real life which we know and have loved, and found so full of interest, despite the suffering it entails. And afterwards? Ah well, all is finished. And so the faith of Christians remains empty of content, because we have not perhaps learnt how to present this other life as it should be presented. But is it possible? An effort at least should be made, and one which takes into account modern cultural advances, and in particular the widespread diffusion of scientific attitudes and outlook. Such an approach could

F

perhaps help us to 'situate' those invisible realities which are the object of our faith. Take for example science-fiction novels. You often find in them the idea of a 'parallel world'; that is to say, a real world but one which never (or only exceptionally) comes into contact with our own; for the Einsteinian theory of time-space reality, taken together with certain other scientific theories, seems to suggest a sort of mysterious existence which is at the limit of our known universe. To be more precise, there is the new scientific theory of 'inclusion'. This affirms that stars of over a given size would undergo such extreme gravitational pressure that their matter would be crushed and, in an instant, disappear. Some scientists go as far as to add that in these circumstances we would no longer know what would happen – for there would be a kind of vanishing of material substance, or perhaps a sort of transposition into a 'parallel world'. I only quote this example to show how attitudes and outlooks change, and how certain comparisons could perhaps help us to understand the existence of another universe in which the Lord is alive, without belonging to our everyday world. Admittedly these are only images or parables, but should we not invent parables of this sort which would speak to our contemporaries?

There is doubt about the reality of the world of angels; many no longer believe in them. Too often angels have been represented under forms which give no idea as to the nature of these stupendous, spiritual beings. Here, again, new imagery must be found. We should have, I believe, a healthy curiosity about the invisible world and things yet to come: a curiosity which would show that we really believe in life with Jesus after death and await the resurrection as something beyond dispute, affecting our individual lives. We feel anguished sometimes at the thought of the future life and ask ourselves how and when this can be. But those who experience no such anguish, who ask no questions, ought they not to consider whether their faith is not perhaps dormant? We profess to believe in these things, but do we believe in them as realities that we will one day experience?

We need to recapture the Apostles' simplicity of outlook. Clearly in their cosmogony and religious thinking there was no problem; Jesus was bound to return. And he was bound to return on the clouds, just as he had departed. In the Apocalyptic writings things yet to come were presented in a language perfectly adapted to the thinking of the Apostles.

We must await Jesus. We shall find him immediately after death, in a way that is beyond the powers of our imagination. Nevertheless we shall have to await the resurrection to be able to share with him life everlasting in all its fullness, because we can only be with Jesus, as man, after our resurrection.

If the death, burial, and Resurrection of our Saviour have
not changed the apparent course of events, nor relations
between persons, they have, nevertheless, brought about an
upheaval in the heart of man or, to be more precise, in the
relationship between man and God. Saint Paul, so close to
these events, has perhaps spoken best. He has tried to make
us understand all that baptism means for us. Dead with
Christ, buried with Christ, we are also risen with Christ.
Numerous texts – some of them difficult to interpret –
speak to us of this drama of man's redemption in Christ:
a drama which Paul himself lived. We live it with him, when
he speaks to us about the struggle between the flesh and the
spirit, death to sin, freedom from the law. Clearly he is
speaking first and foremost out of his own experience.
Hence a number of attitudes and expressions that we have
difficulty in understanding, unless we put ourselves in his
place: in the place of Paul, a Jew, a Pharisee, a follower of a
distinguished rabbi, and a man who had lived in servitude
to the law. But what applies to him applies to us all; his
reaction to the death, burial, and Resurrection of Jesus
makes an impact upon each one of us. We have to live
these mysteries. It is not enough to believe in the Resurrection. We must live it. That is what it means to be a
Christian.

But what significance has the Resurrection for our
present life, from day to day? 'If we are become like him

through a death similar to his,' Saint Paul writes, 'we shall be like him by reason of a similar resurrection. With him, through baptism, we are laid in the tomb: with him, again, we are resurrected.' What counts for Paul is to become a new creature. He shows what this entails: to be clothed in Christ, to be delivered from sin, to find peace and joy in God, to to become a temple of God and of the Holy Spirit, to participate in the fullness and glory of Christ; to be children of God, heirs to the kingdom of heaven, liberated from the spirit of fear and servitude. What does this mean for us in practical terms? Saint Paul tells us that we are dead to sin. Yet we find, in fact, that we are extraordinarily weak, that sin often holds sway over us, that it is very much alive. This problem is the greater in that, in the world today, we cannot talk about the mystery of death or about mortification without stirring up controversy. Some argue that every Christian is already risen with Christ. There has come to light in our times, it seems, a new interpretation of Christianity which maintains that we are already living the resurrection with Jesus, in the freedom of the children of God.

Is it conceivable there could be, in the Church, a kind of progress from one age to the next whereby man would be enabled, while living the demands of Christianity, to see these more and more as an extension of charity, and so to live in much greater freedom, without fear (to the same degree as formerly) of temptations whether of the flesh or of the spirit? Would there, then, no longer be a struggle within us? For Saint Paul speaks of a struggle: the law of the flesh and the law of the spirit are in opposition and the man of the old dispensation is at variance with him who is born anew in Christ. 'Unhappy that I am – who will deliver me from this body of death? I do that which I do not want to do, and what I want to do I fail to do.' I do not see how it can be otherwise for us. Who would be so bold as to declare that there is no longer a struggle between the flesh and the spirit? Saint Paul was painfully aware of temptation. There is even the mysterious text – one that requires perceptive interpretation – which leads us to suppose that there was in his life some sort of set-back to his progress, of a humiliating kind: an angel of Satan buffeted him, and he prayed God that he might be delivered. 'It is in our weakness that the power of God is made manifest,' was the answer he received. We recognize our own struggles in those of Saint Paul, our own temptations in his. And so we ourselves and many of our contemporaries – if we are really to be able to put on Christ and reach the full stature of charity – must consider the question of self-discipline: that is to say, asceticism.

Experience in counselling sincere Christians leads me to the conclusion that forms of asceticism which in the past were beneficial are less so today, and can in certain instances lead to psychological difficulties. Indeed, an asceticism adapted to the conditions of modern life has not yet clearly emerged. The cessation of the Lenten fast and Friday abstinence meant, for many Christians, the end of an obligation that in any case was no longer practised with any enthusiasm. It was obvious that this traditional kind of asceticism had no longer any real relevance today. The truth is modern man is not greatly concerned with food. There are so many people who seldom sit down to a large meal. In modern cities the majority make do with something light, taken in haste in a snack-bar or a self-service café. This is not the level on which to examine the problem of self-discipline which is necessary if we are to follow the Lord; and true Christians feel this instinctively.

On the other hand, if we consider ascetic practices traditionally employed in the monastic life, such as vigils and the use of the discipline, we come to a similar conclusion. To curtail sleep is often a grave imprudence, and some of the difficulties encountered in the religious life or the life of chastity have their origin in nervous exhaustion due to lack of sleep. However, it remains true, for priest and layman alike, that prayer during the night, in union with that of the Lord, can be beneficial. But that is another matter. For it is not an act of asceticism to pray in union with Jesus in the calm of the night. In view of the confusion that at present exists on the question of self-discipline as a condition necessary for Christian perfection, there is still scope, I believe, for a good deal of experimentation as well as much to be learnt in the matter of giving guidance to Christians in the modern world. I am not speaking of men and women who have chosen the monastic life; their separation from the world, together with the basic rhythm of their lives, can allow some of these practices to remain valid – provided, that is, these are adapted to the outlook of persons living today.

A few suggestions on the forms which contemporary asceticism could take are not, I think, out of place. We live in an era when the world presents itself as both beautiful and attractive. It is impossible to say otherwise; there are modern inventions and all sorts of goods at our disposal – the product of intelligence and technical skill. Many of them are admirable. Nor would anyone maintain that there is anything wrong in itself in this increase of products devised by man. However, all this brings into being a different world of which man is the maker. But this new world gives birth, in its turn, to a new kind of man. We have only to look at the young to understand this. The multiplicity of occupations open to them and the countless attractions at their disposal fosters in them a capacity to adapt to situations as they arise – and this is a positive factor. Moreover people are better informed on world affairs, and this results in a genuine sense of the solidarity of mankind. The working class in particular respond readily to appeals that come from the destitute and the afflicted, no matter from what part of the world. This is a remarkable phenomenon. Not a week, not a day, passes without our hearts and sensibilities being harrowed by some form of suffering or disaster, set before our eyes on the television screen. True, gradually people become used to this, as to everything, and there is a risk of the sensibilities being blunted. Yet the feeling of solidarity develops none the less, and that also is a positive element which can foster a charity that is more authentic, more beneficial. We are learning in this way the advantages of mutual aid and how to help one another more effectively, above all in the poorest section of the population. On the other hand, man is worn out by nervous strain. The pace of life is exhausting, and it is impossible to escape noise. Here is a real problem, and something must be done, if a minimum of self-discipline is to be maintained. We must learn to shun noise on certain days, and create within ourselves zones of silence. We must also have the willpower to relax – for relaxation becomes in our times a difficult art, whereas formerly it was a need which one could spontaneously satisfy. Yes, we must learn to relax. And here we have a real form of asceticism, as some families are beginning to discover when they realize the ill-effects arising from the disorderly way in which holidays and times of leisure are planned. Generally it is only a matter of exchanging one form of activity for another. People no longer mind continual travel from place to place. Also, they participate to excess in exhausting sports – which may perhaps lead to a realization that discipline is necessary. Then again, our lives are invaded by audio-visual techniques: the cinema, television, canned music. Many families are faced with the problem as to how to bring up their children in this respect. How is television to be used? Should it be turned off? Should children be taught to make use of it sensibly? This is no easy matter. And then there are those who, because they have a sedentary occupation do not get enough exercise. Others, on the contrary, go in for sport to excess. Of course physical exercise is necessary: we realize the good that come of exercise and the need for it, if we are to relax, avoid nervous tension, and learn self-control. We have here a form of asceticism which can be beneficial.

We live in a world in which publicity is abused: sex appeal, the display of wealth, enticements to spend money, all combine to make slaves of us at every moment. Only a spirit of poverty can enable us to keep ourselves in check and resist these many allurements.

This is not a complete list. But we begin to see a pattern emerging which Christian asceticism could take. The very nature of what we are discussing makes it difficult to formulate a rule, lay down laws. During Lent some limit could be set to the time spent on pleasures, television, or the cinema. But how could this be regulated? In the world today, it rests more and more with the individual to assume responsibility in the matter of asceticism, which, if one is to live as a Christian, remains more than ever necessary. It is, then, a matter of self-discipline. The Christian should behave with the independence and the responsibility of an adult. I do not see how anyone can put himself in another's place – lay down for another, in detail, what he ought to do if he is to use this world, yet not belong to it.

I spoke of the beauty and attraction of so many aspects of the world today. But it must also be said that people become quickly sated with the present way of life. It is amazing to see how some of the young, at twenty years of age, are already, one might say, glutted. They have used and misused music, painting, television, the cinema, sport, leisure, travel: they have tried out everything. This is not true of a minority. We have here, it seems, one of the characteristics of the modern world which is common more or less to all mankind.

But I do not think that we ought to take a pessimistic view of the world today. We should, however, do all in our power to find common ground between the man of the New Dispensation – that is, every Christian baptized in the death and resurrection of Christ, as Saint Paul says – and this modern man fashioned by a civilization which he must learn to dominate, to master. We must find a way to bring the two together. And we must begin by educating ourselves, so that we may learn, in the light of Christ, how to find our way into the heart of such a society.

It could, I think, be helpful to set these realities side by side: on the one hand, the mystery of the death of the Lord and his Resurrection; on the other, the world as it is, with this inner conflict of modern man – a conflict which can only be resolved through participation in the death and Resurrection of Jesus. Should not man live in such a way that he can become fitted to be resurrected one day in the glory of Christ? For want of adequate instruction, too many Christians are perhaps inclined to think that, already participating in the Resurrection of Jesus, they need no longer make the effort to die to self. The resurrection within each one of us is only a seed, as it were, which has to grow. No one can free us from this inner struggle and each time this struggle is abandoned there ensues the degradation of man.

It is after participating in the death of Jesus at the foot of the cross that we can learn to enter into the joy of the risen Christ – this joy which, the Lord has said, no one can take from us. It is a joy which we must foster in our hearts and which will give us hope, courage, and light, which are necessary if we are to face, day after day, the difficulties of life.

11 Priests and Shepherds of Souls with Jesus and in his Church

'It is not you who have chosen me, but I who have chosen you,' Jesus said to his Apostles towards the end of his life. And again: 'I have established you that you may go forth and bear fruit.' If we ponder on the account of the first meetings of Jesus with those who were to become his Apostles we are aware of the emotion felt by these men as they look back on their encounter with their beloved master: the first call.

James and John, with their father Zebedee and his helpers, were fishing on the lake when Jesus came to find them. They knew him already, but this time Jesus said to them: 'Come, follow me, and I will make you fishers of men.' And the two left their father and those with him who were repairing the nets, and followed the Lord.

Much the same happened to Simon Peter, but in Peter's eyes the call was bound up with the miraculous draught of fishes. Indeed, this incident tells us something about his temperament. He is full of enthusiasm, but he is also the victim of misgivings and weaknesses. He is afraid: 'Depart from me Lord, for I am a sinner.' Alarm had overtaken him because they had caught all those fish. As fishermen, they realized that this enormous catch was something out of the ordinary. No sign could have made a greater impact upon them. Their horizon was limited: they had never in their lives been anything except fishermen. 'Fear not,' Jesus said, 'from now on you will be fishers of men.' What did the Lord mean? For these words of Jesus suggest that it is almost easier to catch men than fish. 'Fear not.' And Jesus told Peter, just as he had told the others, that he must leave all.

Next came the calling of Andrew, and then of another, the Evangelist tells us. They were with John the Baptist at the time, whom they had followed as a prophet. 'Behold the lamb of God,' John said to them as Jesus passed by. What, we wonder, did the simple words mean to those who heard them: the Lamb of God? We do not know. But clearly they were strongly attracted by the personality of Christ. They followed him at a distance. Then Jesus turned round. 'What is it you look for?', he asked. And they, not knowing what to say, replied: 'Master, where do you live?' 'Come and see,' Jesus answered. And that was all, on the first evening. But bonds, we feel, had been forged. They admired and loved him whom they had just chosen as their Master. That they were sure they had found the Messiah was clear from the first encounter. 'We have found the Messiah,' Andrew said to Simon Peter. Then Philip, when he too was won over, passed on the message to Nathaniel: 'We have found him of who Moses wrote. He is Jesus, son of Joseph of Nazareth.' We know Nathaniel's reply: 'Can any good thing come out of Nazareth?' 'Come and see,' was Philip's simple answer. Come and see. That was enough. Jesus had only to look at Nathaniel and speak to him. Nathaniel at once replied: 'You are the Son of God, you are the king of Israel.'

Their faith was far from complete, but it is striking that, as soon as they were called, they followed Jesus. Some came because the message had been passed on to them. Others were called personally by the Lord. This happened to Matthew as he sat at the seat of custom. Jesus passed by and said to him: 'Come.' And Matthew got up, brought Jesus to his house, and gave him a meal along with the others.

This first call to the apostolate took, then, a variety of

forms. The essential point is that those who were called followed Jesus and had to leave all else to follow him. Did they leave everything, once and for all? Or was it their intention simply to follow the Master on the occasions when he was preaching, as people used to follow a prophet as he went from place to place? We do not know. Doubtless the Apostles themselves did not know immediately.

But the Apostles were not alone in following Jesus. They were joined by many others: disciples who also followed Jesus and were united to him by a like attachment, a like eagerness to hear his teaching. To the Apostles, however, there was extended a kind of second invitation. 'Jesus went away on to a mountain to pray, and he passed all the night in prayer to God. And when it was day he summoned his disciples and chose twelve of them whom he called Apostles.' He spent all the night in converse with his Father, in contemplation of his Father, before choosing his Apostles. Now we understand the words he spoke towards the end of his life: 'Father, those whom you have given to me . . .' The Apostles were, in fact, given by God to Jesus, and Jesus called them.

Then came the three years which the Apostles passed in the company of their Master. The Apostles were not always quick in the up-take. Also, they were often, it seems, attached to human ways of thinking. We can see from time to time, from some remark let fall by the Lord, that they must have made 'heavy weather': that they must have been slow to understand, to grasp a point. At moments the Lord seems almost to lose patience with them. To think that those men who had been chosen by Jesus, who had lived in his company, who had come to know him, who had followed him, who had heard his teaching, who had been moulded and remoulded by him time and again – to think that these same men sometimes, it seems, tried the patience of the Lord by their slowness to understand and to change their ways! For ourselves, this is a reassuring thought.

Today, as then, the same Providence watches over us. Jesus did not perform a miracle to change the temperaments of his Apostles: he did not forestall the slow working of grace – the slow emergence of the spiritual life. And yet he chose these as his Apostles, and destined them to become the pillars of the Church. We imagine, sometimes, that the Holy Spirit on the day of Pentecost transformed the Apostles turning them into supermen. God did indeed make them capable of being the pillars of the Church, but he left them their weaknesses, their faults, their temptations, their ordinary way of life; and it is through all this that the power of God is revealed.

The Apostles passed the test of the Passion, which for them was the test of their faith in Jesus, the Son of God. It is above all through the death of Jesus that they began to participate in the design of God. The reproach addressed to Peter: 'You think as men think,' shows us this. Yes, Peter thought as men think, not as God thinks, whereas Jesus had to fulfil the design of God. When, we wonder, did the Apostles begin to think as God thought? The test presented by the death of Jesus was distressing for Peter, above all. Did he show himself weaker than the others who had fled? Precisely because they fled, they were not exposed to the temptation of weakness. Peter at least had tried to follow. He followed from a distance. He went as far as the courtyard of the High Priest's house. There, when he was questioned, he took fright and denied his Master.

Moreover, there is a link between this betrayal and the amazing scene of the second call to Peter, on the shore of Lake Tiberias: 'Peter, do you love me?' We know the three-fold answer which revealed Peter's distress at the insistence on the part of his Master, who seemed to have some doubt as to Peter's fidelity. That is why, apparently, Jesus reminded him that not so long ago he had given the same assurances. Is he still so sure of himself?

In the light of the story – so brief but admirable – of the

call to the Apostles we should ask ourselves about our own
calling. Have we really been called? What, basically is a
vocation? Perhaps we remember the hour or the day when
we heard the first invitation from Jesus, when in all our
fervour, all our joy of heart, all the generosity of adolescence,
we felt, without any doubt whatsoever, that Jesus was calling us. And then the years passed. Does Jesus still call us?
Did he ever call us at all? Is not the feeling of having a
vocation the product of our imagination? For in this sphere,
above all, where the senses are involved, we need certainty.
We cannot be satisfied by illusions: we cannot built our
lives on a dream which we would like to come true. Life
is hard, and in difficulties we are brought face to face
with ourselves. Have we the right to affirm that we have
been personally chosen by Jesus, called by name? If it is
true that Jesus has called us, then his call remains un-
changed – for it would be a human way of thinking to visu-
alize this calling in terms of time. The time of the Lord is not
our time. His call rings out for ever: it is eternal, even as he
himself is eternal. It is our response that can change, differ
from one day to the next: we have to answer his call anew
every day.

But can we be certain? To ask this is to broach the whole
question of the Providence of God and a personal relationship between the Lord and each one of us. We come back
always to the same point. When we consider the Church,
its tradition, its teaching, as well as the experiences of the
vast number who bear witness to the Lord, including those
who have been called to share in his priesthood; when we
reflect, in simple faith and complete confidence, upon all
that God tells us on this matter, we cannot doubt. No one,
I believe, can follow the apostolic or religious vocation
without having been called to do so by the Lord, and this
calling, because it binds us individually to the person of
Christ, is something different from Providence which in a
general way governs the whole of creation. Perhaps it is

different even from the relations between the Saviour and each one whom he has redeemed, for there seems to be, in the case of a vocation, a gratuitous choice on the part of Christ: a decision freely made by Jesus – one that is free, with all the freedom of friendship. The Lord wanted us and chose us for his friends, for it is not possible to be called to the apostolate without our being among his friends.

Now we come to the vital question. What does 'a friend of Jesus' mean? And how do we respond to this mark of preference? What Jesus demands unwearyingly from his Apostles is confidence. Yes, confidence. He asks that they should have no fear. And if Jesus submitted Peter to a test of confidence, in calling to him to walk on the storm-tossed waters, it is because this has much to teach us. Peter responded. In his enthusiasm he wanted to be with the Lord at once, without delay. But he did not yet understand the demands implicit in a love such as this for his master. That is why, once again, he was afraid. It is this kind of fear which harms our vocation, this timidity in the face of all that is involved when we have to follow Jesus; fear as to our commitments when we give ourselves, in a concrete way, to the service of God; fear, too, of difficulties, present and to come.

Once we have really grasped what it means to be called by the Lord, and moreover, that this call is permanent, speaking to us each day, each hour, we must learn that it demands a response which is always changing. We change as the years pass, and our inner self changes, too. But the growth of a unique friendship with the Son of man, our Master and Saviour, must be strengthened and deepened within the concrete reality of our lives. And if we seem to have lost sight of this demand made by friendship, it is always possible to listen anew to the call of Jesus and respond to it, for the Lord is faithful to his choice: the bonds of his friendship are eternal.

*

The apostolic vocation demands, above all, a radical detachment from the world, from creation. Now, we will not be truly free, with the freedom necessary for the service of the Lord, unless we are detached not only from the world but from ourselves. The apostle should be in the world, yet not of the world. The Lord himself told us this: 'I have left you in the world, but you are not of the world.' And to reassure us in our difficulties, he added: 'I have overcome the world.' Now, we cannot be in the world without being of the world, unless we model ourselves on the Lord, unless we learn to overcome the world as he did – and that meant renunciation of self and death upon the cross.

Another trait of the apostolate is that it requires us to be instruments of the Lord. The apostolate is not our doing: we are in the service of the Lord and the work in which we are involved goes beyond all human work – beyond, too (this is important) the sphere of personal success. Detachment from the world would be vain if it did not lead to a detachment from our activities. For the danger that continually lies in wait for us in apostolic work is that of yielding to the need, natural to man, to feel himself the master of his activities. Now in the apostolate we are not entitled to be our own masters. The apostolate is a work of the Lord in the Church: a work of the Holy Spirit in souls and in the world. We cannot be masters of what has only been entrusted to us. This perhaps is the most difficult thing in a human life: to give, completely, with all the resources of our intelligence, our hearts, and our energy, while remaining (as far as results are concerned) free – poor, that is, in the sense in which the world is used in the Beatitudes. This humble detachment is the more important because the apostolate demands the employment of some of the highest qualities in man. If, in administering the sacraments, the qualities of the priest, in so far as he is performing his priestly duties, do not directly influence the nature and the fruits of this sacramental ministry, it is not the same

G

thing when it comes to spreading the Gospel. This makes the apostolate a serious and difficult matter. Indeed, in approaching the tasks which, in their many forms, are directed to this end – to the spreading of the faith, the teaching of truths revealed in the Gospel, the guidance of the faithful – we should be aware that we are faced with, humanly speaking, one of the most difficult tasks imaginable. When we have to speak in the name of the Lord, give direction in his name, we should do this in the greatest humility of heart and mind, aware of our inadequacy, our inexperience, our faults – strong solely in the power of the Lord.

This spirit of service, this feeling of entire dependence on Christ and complete detachment in relation to the mission which has been entrusted to us in the Church – this ought to bestow on us the attitude and outlook of a humble servant who expects nothing for himself. Jesus, indeed, said that he did not call us servants, but friends. But he also told his Apostles not to exercise authority in the manner of temporal rulers; not to allow themselves to be addressed as 'master' or 'teacher'. Before he died, he wanted, when he washed the feet of the Apostles, to remind them, by a gesture upon which the nearness of his Passion conferred the importance and solemnity of a last testament, that, in carrying out their mission, they should behave as humble servants. The Apostles had disputed among themselves as to which of them would have the first place. Jesus, who read their thoughts, rebuked them. 'What were you saying among yourselves? What were you discussing as you went along?' And when, embarrassed and shamed, they dared not reply, he said: 'He who wishes to be first will be the last among you and the servant of all.'

One of the most important requirements in the apostolic mission is revealed by Jesus when he takes as an example the true shepherd. 'I know my sheep, and my sheep know me.' The shepherd must know his sheep. Yes, it is perhaps on the level of this mutual understanding between shepherd and sheep that one of the greatest difficulties in the apostolate arises. The shepherd should know his sheep. What knowledge have we of those to whom we have to preach the Gospel? The Church cannot be merely a teaching organization like any other. Nor can it be an organization, like so many, for spreading propaganda. No, it is the faith that it must communicate: a living faith. It is the faith that it must teach, and before being masters who teach others, we must ourselves give witness to what it is we teach. And this witness presupposes a contact, in deep humility, with those to whom we are sent. Moreover we cannot teach independently of the Holy Spirit. No attempt to spread the Gospel, no proclamation of belief, can achieve anything, unless the Holy Spirit is at work in the depths of our hearts. This is indeed so, though all may appear to be taking place on a purely natural level. Another point. If Jesus himself did not at once succeed in what we could call the formation of his Apostles; if, as I have suggested, he sometimes found them heavy-going, how can we aspire to be more successful than he? And Jesus had only a few to mould, whereas we are often concerned with thousands of persons, whole areas of our cities. It is, indeed, a momentous task and one that needs delicate handling. And furthermore it is all too true that we do not know, as we should, those to whom we proclaim the faith.

When we reflect on the Church in its immensity, when we see on one side the world and humanity, and on the other the little meagre band of those who spread the message of the Lord, we wonder what we should do to enable such an apostolate to function. People are less ready to be taught today than they were in the past. They are less ready, too, to accept the faith when presented by means of instructions addressed to large gatherings. They like to make personal contact with – if possible, to meet one at a time – those who bring the message of the Lord. Yes, the shepherd must know his sheep, and his sheep know him.

We have to remind ourselves again and again that we do not know those to whom we are speaking. We think, perhaps, that we know them; or we know them in a general, abstract kind of way. It is the duty, then, of each one of us to decide for himself how best to acquire the knowledge that is lacking, to accept responsibility in this field. It is a matter which should preoccupy us all and one which demands, I repeat, great humility.

We must have, too, an intimate knowledge of the truth which it is our duty to communicate. For to proclaim the message of God – which, as I have stressed, appears so improbable, so unbelievable, to our contemporaries – we must ourselves be convinced, beyond all shadow of doubt, that this message is nothing less than the deposit of revealed truth. The apostle must have a calm certainty that what he has proclaimed to others he has himself received from God. This presupposes a personal assimilation of the truths of the faith. I have heard it said that we should preach theology. Experience has led me to think otherwise. Theology is a science. No, we ought not to preach theology, but we ought to have so assimilated its content that we are able to preach the Lord with certainty and clarity while – going beyond knowledge acquired by the study of theology – we at the same time speak of these invisible, supernatural realities as if we had actually experienced and seen them. We should be able to put ourselves into the hearts and minds of those who are listening: to know their problems; their sufferings, their intellectual limitations – to understand what, for them, can be the point of departure that will set them on the way to faith. This is impossible if we are not in close contact with others. And we cannot draw closer to them simply because we know something. If we teach in an authoritarian tone, we will not be listened to. We must be, at the same time, both convinced witnesses and human beings capable of approaching our fellow-men.

This problem of getting to know people is of major im-

portance today. It presupposes, as well as humility of heart
and openness of mind, certain gifts which (let us not be
afraid to admit this) all of us do not possess. Yes, we need
the natural gifts of intuition, imagination, and the art of
presenting the truths which we wish to be understood. We
must have no illusions about this for here lies the mystery
of the Church. If every priest is able to learn to celebrate
the Eucharist with devotion and to administer the sacraments, not every priest is equally capable of preaching the
Gospel, even though in other respects he may have excellent qualities. This is a fact which we must face. We have
come across much suffering among certain priests who felt
that they were failures, men who lacked intuition and the
'feeling' for teaching. Yes, it is indeed a mystery in the
Church how the charism of the Holy Spirit works, as a
rule, upon natural gifts, but rarely takes their place. There is,
it is true, a level of sanctity, union with the Lord, and contemplation, which transcend all else. But this is exceptional.
When we think that the Lord entrusted the expansion of the
Church, the teaching of the faith, and the guidance of
hearts, to men much like all others – some of them suited
to their task, others less so – we understand better the nature
of the Church and the poverty of the means at its disposal.
Even among the Apostles, although they were endowed
with the charism of the Holy Spirit, their ability to spread
the Gospel differed. There were blunders, and arguments
between them. Paul and a companion had to part because
they disagreed. All we have been told about the early Church
helps us to realize that, when it came to actual preaching,
things were far from easy.

The certainty that we have the help of the Spirit promised by Jesus does not permit us to underestimate the
tasks entrusted to us. But we must not lose heart. On the
contrary, we have every reason to be confident. But we must
be humble. People cannot bear priests who are too sure of
themselves. The main difficulty lies in the fact that we

must be wholly true to the teaching of the faith, and yet be able to address those who are far from ready to accept his teaching in the form we ourselves received it. Should we speak, then, of the need to adapt our presentation of the faith? I do not like the term 'adapt', but, for want of a better one, we have to use it. Be that as it may, we are sometimes disconcerted by a reluctance on the part of the faithful to accept certain realities or attitudes relating to the faith. What is at issue here? Some priests in their concern, as shepherds of souls, to make themselves acceptable and intelligible, are tempted to think, as soon as what they say is rejected, that they must therefore find something else to say. Hence the problem of how to present knowledge objectively and the faith in a way that can be understood. We must recognize humbly our responsibility in this field, and reflect whether we have, in fact, learnt to present the faith with objectivity – as it really is. This is a difficult task, if viewed purely on the natural plane. The thought of the qualities needed to carry it out fills us with dismay. But it is no use living in a state of illusion. We need, I repeat once more, much humility, much faith – but a faith that is assimilated and lived in a way that puts us to the test, making us ask ourselves how we can pass on to others the beliefs by which we ourselves live. Above all we have to learn to understand the minds and hearts of those to whom we speak.

Here we are touching on one of the demands of the apostolic life which – especially in the world today – seems beyond our powers, unless, that is, we are, at least to some degree genuine contemplatives. For, as I have already remarked, only a personal experience of God can give to our words a conviction that will touch men's hearts. Yes, words must reflect in all sincerity our personal experience. This, at any rate, is what our contemporaries feel. Anyone who adopts a professorial tone, or teaches with a suave assurance, or take liberties with the content of the faith under the pretext of adaptation, is simply not listened to. Man is looking for something else. Whether he knews it or not, he is looking for the absolute.

12 The Poor with Jesus of Nazareth

Our contemplation of Jesus as master and model of the Apostles would be incomplete if we did not speak about poverty: the poverty of the Apostles of Jesus and of his Church. It is, I must admit, a formidable subject, as well as being a complicated one. It may appear strange, at first sight, that the virtue the purpose of which is to simplify man's life, to set him, stripped of all things, face to face with God; to leave him wholly free to draw nearer to God, should in practice raise such great problems – ones, moreover, which will not cease to present themselves because they will never be completely solved.

The difficulty arises from the fact that the word 'poverty' is used in different senses. Those who talk about it do not always speak the same language. The world speaks one language, Christ speaks another, while we sometimes use a third. At one time we mean by poverty the virtue of detachment. At another it is a question of poverty in the ordinary sense of the word: privation which many people suffer – something hateful which the majority of the poor try to avoid and resist. Then again, the word is used of the vow taken by religious. The same word, therefore is applied to realities that are entirely different.

Furthermore, poverty is relative to the standard of living in a society, and the struggle to escape from it takes place under cultural, political and social régimes that differ one from another. It is hard, therefore to speak of poverty without reference to the régime under which man works. But, whatever the context, all these régimes, political and social, exist to procure for men the largest possible number of material benefits. That is why, when we try to raise the question of possessing or utilizing the products of this world, with a view to the kingdom of God and in accordance with the teachings of the Gospel, we come up against difficulties. There is the risk that either we shall remain on the theoretical or abstract plane or else fail to be understood.

If we consider, from the theological point of view, the three counsels of perfection, which according to tradition constitute the basis of the religious life – that is to say: obedience, chastity, and poverty – we give obedience the first place. Obedience indeed constitutes and demonstrates in practice the most complete gift that a free, intelligent creature can make of self to his Creator. This gift contains and brings with it the others. Chastity follows in second place. Then, finally, poverty, which is on the level of detachment from material possessions. Now, it is remarkable that in general usage the order of these values is in reverse. As Christians we begin with the highest: we put, first, freedom of will; then freedom of heart; and, lastly, freedom in the matter of earthly possessions. The world attaches most importance to possessions. Perhaps that is why it particularly appreciates poverty in the religious life. Indeed, it attaches an over-riding importance to poverty. As to chastity, it is not of much interest, even when it is believed possible, and that is not always the case. When it comes to obedience, not only is it thought of as having no value – it is considered, indeed, to be 'opting out' of responsibility on the part of man and, consequently, as an evil or, at best, a state of imperfection. It is in the face of this confusion of values that we have to reflect on the idea of poverty.

To put some order into our reflections, let us consider, in

turn, Jesus, the Church, and the world. I do not claim to offer solutions to these problems, only to make some suggestions as to the first steps we might take if we are to help the Church to grow in poverty in accordance with Christ and thus conform the more to what the Lord expects of us. Let us take first the poverty of Jesus of Nazareth. The reality in this case is simple. It is, however, of the utmost importance that we should know how Jesus lived at Nazareth. For, if Providence directs all things, it is clear that the way of life chosen by the Word made Flesh is not without significance – specially as it extended over a period of thirty years. What we are considering, therefore, is how Christ lived on earth: his status in relation to society and the family. Now, we are struck, above all, by his self-effacement: he was one of many – much like anyone else. His was not a condition of extreme poverty: it was the poverty that goes with hard work, as is the case for the vast majority of human beings. Extreme poverty – amounting to destitution – would have meant that his way of life was exceptional. When the census was held and Mary and Joseph had to find a lodging at Bethlehem they were lost in the crowd. Mary was only one woman among many, and when they lodged in a stable hewn out of rock, they were sharing the lot of numerous families. That Jesus worked with his hands to provide for himself and his family was perfectly natural: it could not have been otherwise. He did not leave Nazareth. He did not engage in special studies. He did not belong to the tribe of Levi. He had no priestly privilege. He was, however, of the tribe of David.

We must not be too influenced by our present ideas, when we consider society as it was in Israel in the time of the Lord. I do not think we should speak, in the case of Jesus, of poverty on the social level. What matters for us is to remember that Jesus was poor, in the sense in which the word poverty is ordinarily used. And this is important. For Jesus in becoming man, wanted to live in accordance with the conditions then prevalent, until the time came for him to manifest himself and enter upon his prophetic and Messianic mission. Up to that moment he lived the life of the poor – life as it is lived by the vast majority of those who are born, work for a living, found a family, die. They live a completely ordinary life: they do not have interesting tasks to perform, their names are unknown. Most of them do not shine in any apostolic work: they are too poor, too humble for that. They are simply human beings. What Jesus reveals by the life he chose is the dignity of man, of every man, simply because he is a man – every man who has been born, who has tried to live as best he can in poverty and anonymity, who has died without any reason for him to be remembered. It was God's plan that Jesus should live on this obscure level in Israel, and at Nazareth: a town which had not a good reputation. And this shows beyond question that all perfection which comes from God, all the perfection of a child of God, can be attained in the ordinary life lived by any human being. For Mary it was the same; she was simply the mother of her son, which is the lot of countless women who have lived solely for their family. We have here the unfathomable mystery of Nazareth. From this we should learn respect for the poor: respect for those who have no influence, no name in the world. We should believe that Christian perfection in all its fullness is within reach of these, for they can be perfect as Jesus was perfect at Nazareth.

*

We must reflect for a moment on the attitude of Jesus in regard to wealth and poverty: his teaching on this. His attitude, as reflected in the Gospels, is characterized by a sovereign liberty in the face of all things, and this finds particular expression in his public and apostolic life. Jesus had nothing: he possessed nothing, but he did not refuse what was offered to him. He told those who wanted to

follow him that if 'the foxes had holes and the birds of
the air nests, the Son of man has nowhere to lay his head.'
And the meaning of these words goes far beyond anything
one might suppose. Jesus had no occupation as the world
understands it; he had no home as the world understands
it, neither as prophet nor as Messiah. He belonged to his
calling. He belonged to all mankind. He was the property,
as it were, of the entire human race. He was for all men.
He associated with the rich as well as with the poor, whom
he understood and preferred, for he knew what was in the
heart of man and he made no exception of persons. He
lived from day to day. Women followed him and served
him. He and those in his company pooled their resources.
He lodged with one, ate with another. We have here all the
liberty of the apostle. And when he sent out his disciples
he said to them: 'Take nothing for your journey, neither
staff nor sack nor bread nor money. In whatever house
you enter, stay . . .'

The most important teaching of Jesus on poverty is
found in the Sermon on the Mount, in the Beatitudes:
'Happy are the poor in heart,' or 'Happy are the poor,'
as another evangelist puts it. But I doubt whether we can
speak of one Beatitude – that of poverty – apart from the
others. The more we try to understand the meaning of
the Beatitudes, the more we realize that they cannot be
separated one from another; they form a whole. It is not
possible to live one of them without living all; and they can
be lived only in love. The Beatitudes are a kind of code,
showing how to love God. It is not easy, then, to speak about
the Beatitudes. They are to be lived rather than explained.
It must be observed, however, that the Lord promised
happiness. 'Happy.' We have, here, the happiness that no
one can demonstrate or explain on the rational level. It is
the happiness which is enjoyed by those who have committed themselves to live by these same Beatitudes: the
happiness of poverty, thirst, tears, persecution – the hap-

piness of gentleness, humility, compassion, and the works of peace.

We are far removed here from a simple definition as to what should be our attitude to money. That is why it is perhaps important to note the sternness with which the Lord speaks of riches. In the presence of those endowed with this world's goods, one is confounded to the point of being unable to read the words: 'Cursed be the rich, for you have your reward.' We can soften them down, say that they apply only to the rich who are evil. Nevertheless, it seems that, in the mind of the Lord, wealth is indeed thought of as being in some way dangerous, even if we are only remotely associated with it. 'You cannot serve God and money.' To serve money. 'Truly, I say to you, it will be hard for the rich man to enter into the Kingdom of Heaven . . . Yes, I say to you again and again, it is easier for a camel to pass through the eye of a needle than for a rich man to enter into the Kingdom of Heaven.' I know Christians, men of faith, who have been devastated by these words of Christ, which pose for them a serious problem. I do not think we have the right to minimize the importance of the words of Jesus, they are written in Holy Scripture until the end of time. On the other hand we see with what naturalness Jesus frequented the company of some of the rich, and the delicacy he showed to Zacchaeus, who had, nevertheless, amassed wealth by wrongful means. Let us recall how Jesus treats him – with what kindness and compassion: singling him out before the whole town, visiting his home, for Zacchaeus had repented, resolved to make amends and restore to those whom he had injured a larger sum than he had extorted from them. The attitude of Jesus to the poor is revealed in simple gestures, allusions, words he lets fall that show his sympathy for them and his deep understanding. We have already recalled his exclamation of wonder when the widow dropped her small coin into the treasury of the Temple. In the sight of God she had given her all.

'The poor have the Gospel preached to them,' Jesus replied to those sent by John to show him that the kingdom of the Messiah was near. 'The poor have the Gospel preached to them.' What exactly did the Lord mean by these words? Did he mean that the message of the Gospel is addressed in a particular manner to the poor? Did he mean that the Good News, thus proclaimed, is especially directed to the poor, so as to give them hope and happiness? I think there is something more in these words – namely, that all who preach the Gospel should be able to make it intelligible to the poor. 'The poor have the Gospel preached to them . . .' We shall have to come back to this saying of the Lord.

*

Let us consider for a moment the saints who have followed Jesus especially closely, embracing poverty with a particular austerity – with the folly born of love and with a boundless joy. This reveals another aspect of poverty – something indeed which surpasses poverty as we normally understand it. Let us consider Saint Francis of Assisi and Charles de Foucauld. Saint Francis of Assisi is poor, but it is a poverty that is all joy. It overflows into a tenderness for God's creatures. It is bohemian in spirit. It proclaims the Lord in a spirit of complete freedom. We have here a form of poverty which comes perhaps nearest to that of the times of the Apostles. But the saints who embrace the poverty of Christ in this way are looking for something else besides the freedom of detachment. Along with poverty they deliberately seek out humiliation – what Charles de Foucauld called 'abjection'. It is an expression of a need to conform to the likeness of Christ crucified. In the souls of the saints everything rests on an over-riding need to love and to prove this love. This helps us to understand why the stigmata were imprinted on the hands and feet and heart of Saint Francis, the man of poverty: his poverty was the outpouring of an immense love, a love that went to the lengths of folly.

Yes, all this is contrary to reason. And when Charles de Foucauld at Nazareth wrote that he was flooded with joy because, when he appeared clad in absurd garments, urchins in the streets threw stones at him and mocked him, he was being neither reasonable nor prudent. But he was overwhelmed with joy because, he says, he was small and despised in the town in which Jesus once had lived as a poor man.

We are a long way, here, from the problem of poverty as it is normally presented to us. Folly of this kind, endured for the love of the Lord, is a mystery: it is a way by which we cannot travel unless we are invited by the Holy Spirit.

*

Finally, a word about poverty as the Church teaches and practises it: this will allow us to see better the problems which present themselves today.

First of all it is clear that poverty, in the sense of detachment, has been taught by the Lord as indispensable to Christians – particularly those who want to consecreate their lives to God. Detachment of heart (what is called the 'virtue of poverty') cannot be completely sincere or efficacious if it is not accompanied by a minimum of poverty in the ordinary sense of the word. Unless I am mistaken, the Lord taught that no Christian worthy of the name could be content with detachment of heart, while continuing to live, without scruple, in affluence. He must aim at a life in which poverty has a greater part – while still conforming with the requirements of his position, his family, and profession, and in obedience, also, to the promptings of grace.

There is, too, the religious vow of poverty. Rightly or wrongly the faithful are often scandalized – for the word 'poverty' is used here in a different sense. 'Religious,' they say, 'take a vow of poverty, but their ife is not always poor in the true meaning of the word.' That is what many of the faithful think. And there is some truth in this: for religious do, in fact, take a vow of poverty, but they do not live as the poor live – not, that is to say, as the word poverty is generally understood. The poverty of religious cannot be compared with that of the lowest paid worker or the casual labourer. The vow of poverty, as we know, is a commitment to strip ourselves of all things with the purpose of rooting out of our hearts the desire for possessions. It is a spiritual and juridical renunciation to the right of possession, a commitment to conform to a life of this kind. True, as we have said in regard to detachment, this way of life should be accompanied by a minimum of 'real' poverty. I have said 'real' because in the same phrase I have used the word poverty in two different senses: I could have spoken of material or actual poverty.

The vow of poverty taken by religious can only be realized in a community: the renunciation by a religious of his rights of possession is only made possible if all things are shared in common. Here another problem presents itself, not only on the level of the religious life, but on that of the Church and its apostolic organizations. The Church and its apostles must live: they need resources. The needs of the churches in the mission field, the needs associated with worship, are often considerable. The problem has, of course, existed since the time of the Apostles. The Lord himself, during his public life, lived on gifts made by his disciples, and on the hospitality of those who were accustomed to make a generous offering to any man of God. Jesus, quite naturally, assumed in society the role expected of a prophet. Similarly we know that Paul and the primitive Church lived either on gifts freely bestowed by the faithful or on contributions organized by the Apostles as they went from town to town, or payments for manual work; it depended on circumstances. All this was spontaneous. But we should bear in mind that the Church did not then – to the best of our knowledge – own either property or capital. We know how in the Middle Ages the abuse of revenues and benefices met with a reaction in the form of mendicant Orders – as well as apostolic work undertaken by individuals. And the same problem recurs throughout history, in different circumstances.

How, then, does the Church stand today in the matter of apostolic poverty? We are well aware how things are. There are dioceses which have property and revenues, and there are poor dioceses. There are gifts that the faithful make spontaneously; others that they give because they are asked to do so. There are religious who live from revenues, others on gifts and collections. There are missionaries who have cultural commitments and other involvements. To complicate matters, there is an immense gulf which continues to increase, between the standard of living of rich countries and that of developing countries. And this gap is accentuated in poor countries, whether consciously or unconsciously, by missionaries who belong to rich nations.

It can indeed be difficult on the apostolic level. The priest who comes from one of the rich countries brings with him his own standard of living, even if he himself lives in poverty and simplicity. To add to this, there are lavishly constructed churches, mission centres, institutions, motherhouses, residences for papal nuncios, seminaries. On the material and economic level, things in the Church can be very complicated. We should give thought to this. It is of no avail to talk only of poverty of heart, poverty in the apostolate. We have to bear in mind how the Church appears in the eyes of mankind. Anyone who attempts to preach the Gospel today, particularly among the poor, cannot dissociate himself from the image presented by the Church to the world. This raises a problem that cries out for a solu-

H

tion – for on it depends, to a large extent, whether the Church will be able to spread the message of the Gospel among men of our times.

13   The Poor with Jesus of Nazareth
(continued)

At no period of its history has the Church had to face more questions from the world than in our own times. This is an hour of great importance for the Church, in that all men seem in a more or less confused kind of way, to expect something from it, and sometimes on a plane which has, in fact, nothing to do with the Church, for the demands come as much from the atheistic and unbelieving world as from Christians. From every side much is expected from the Church.

To understand these demands from the world we must remember that ours is an era in which has emerged what can be called the world of the workers: the product of the development of industry and conditions that ensue from this. Now, the world of the workers is steeped, in general, in a materialistic or socialistic way of thinking, which is often atheistic. Furthermore, as well as this world of the workers, there is developing another world, still more poor, which occupies immense areas of the earth. This latter world, which is made up of the poor is, to a greater or lesser degree, aware of its poverty, its aspirations, and its unity. Moreover it is at one in its hope that things can be changed by means of a revolution. In the face of the demands coming from the world of the workers, combined with those from the under-developed countries, the Church is no longer recognized as being able to offer a solution. On the contrary it is thought actually to constitute an obstacle to progress. To those who put their hopes in the establishment of a socialist régime, the Church appears to be bound up with capitalism and imperialism, to both of which it gives – so it is believed – moral support, even if it does not explicitly intend to do so. It is true that the Church has on a number of occasions denounced the abuses and injustices of capitalist systems, but the existence of the Church remains a fact, and what is wanted from it is action. Moreover this has bearing on the need for the Church to give witness to poverty, and carry out its mission in the world of the poor.

Side by side with the demands from the world there are those that come from Christians. Here different tendencies are apparent, all of which, in one way or another, suggest that the Church should be more spiritual, more poor, more impregnated with the spirit of the Gospel – true, not every demand that is made conforms to a right conception of the nature of the Church and the requirements of its mission as intended by its founder. Furthermore, it is desirable, it is felt, that the apostolate should be relieved of certain economic and material pressures and that the institutional side of the Church should give a greater example of poverty. At other periods in its history similar problems have faced the Church, but today these assume such magnitude that all who are charged with the apostolate are obliged to come to grips with them.

*

We should at least suggest along what lines the solution ought to be sought, for we are in duty bound to listen to these demands and to meet them in a spirit of unselfishness. It is true the ideal cannot be attained, yet we must make an effort in that direction. We must come down to the level of concrete proposals. This being so, we will consider in turn: personal poverty, poverty in relation to property and institutions and, finally, poverty in regard to means employed in the apostolate.

On the level of the individual – for example, clergy, priests, apostles, religious (both men and women) – the problem can appear less complex. Poverty as lived by these should be free of all affectation, but it should be genuine poverty. I say this because people do not always recognize poverty as such. I am thinking, for instance, of certain convents where the nuns live a life of selfless poverty, but there is no external sign bearing witness to this. Even if, in their way of life, there is nothing inconsistent with the ideal set before religious, we ought to give thought to the authenticity of the sign. We must avoid anything which can cause misunderstanding — this can be an obstacle to the kingdom of Christ and can deter some from belief in the Church.

Again, on the personal level, understanding of the poor is important. Yes, a cordial, straight-forward understanding of the poor. We cannot separate the practice of poverty from love of the poor. It is distressing beyond words to find the gulf, the wall, which in some places, in some *milieux*, separates the poor from those who proclaim the message of the Gospel. Why can they not understand each other? Why? It is not always poverty itself that is at issue. Some priests are painfully astonished to find that the workers think of them as rich, whereas they are living a life that is poor and austere, and spending less than a worker. How does this come about? It is a question of a difference of outlook and a lack of understanding. A poor man, a worker, who comes to a priest, belongs to a different world: his attitudes, his reactions, his judgments, all are different. Moreover this can make priests feel embarrassed and diffident when they have to deal with the poor. They are not at ease among them: they do not speak the same language, and some things they say give offence to the poor, nor are their reactions the same as theirs. We must face this fact, for we cannot abandon preaching the Gospel to the poor, and if a problem of this nature presents itself to priests charged with the spreading of the Gospel, it must be solved. All too often priests feel deeply this inability to communicate with the workers and the poor.

The solution is indeed not always easy to find. We can blame the formation given to clerics and the often exclusively intellectual *milieu* in which they have been prepared for the priesthood. Yes, the majority of them are ill at ease in the world of the poor and the workers. But we must learn to put ourselves in the place of these poor. We must learn to have a fellow-feeling for them. And that is impossible if we do not participate in their lives, their preoccupations, their concerns. Sometimes everything sets us apart from them. We do not read the same paper, we do not associate with the same people, we have not the same political reactions: what touches the hearts of the masses, leaves us unmoved; on the other hand what is of interest to them is of no interest to us. The poor are uncomplicated and they feel we do not really understand their problems. We think we understand them, but ours is an intellectual knowledge – not knowledge that comes from experience. We tend to treat their problems in an off-hand manner. We are quick to hand out words of comfort, when we have no idea how heavy is the burden of their lives day in and day out. It is not enough that the priest should live a life that is poor on the material level: this poverty must involve real contact with the poor. But contact in itself is not enough. There must be friendship, which means a degree of sharing. Why should priests and religious not feel at home in the world of the workers? It is insufferable that those who bring the message of the Gospel should be, because of their outlook and often the training they have received, strangers in the eyes of the poor. This is the problem. The Church cannot leave this unresolved. We must search for a solution. We must find out why the hopes of the poor have little in common with our conventional way of looking at things. Yes, the poor are inclined to be revolutionaries because they possess nothing, because their patience is at an end, and they deeply resent the injustice they have to suffer. Let us keep watch on ourselves and be honest in examining our conscience. Are we not instinctively on the side of the rich and those who have great possessions, even if this is not our intention? Whether we like it or not, society and the world are divided. There are the rich on one side, the poor on the other. There are rich peoples and poor peoples. There are economic and social systems that are favourable to the rich, and those favourable to the poor. Too often the vast majority of priests and religious do not understand the outlook of the poor and, consequently, judge them harshly because, *a priori*, and as a result of their background, they prefer society as it is – the established order. I am well aware that this question leads us to another. Can the Church, through its priests and religious, learn to think as the poor think, share the feelings and the all too human aspirations of the poor?

In the Church the question of poverty presents itself on the level of buildings. This is more important than one imagines. Most people derive their impressions of the clerical or religious life from externals, which include buildings. Charles de Foucauld writes at the beginning of his Rule: 'Buildings leave their mark on those who live in them.' This is profoundly true. I have never felt it more strongly than when I visited the small, primitive Franciscan monasteries as planned by Saint Francis himself. The same applies to the hermitages of Charles de Foucauld. These simple buildings have a beauty that is humble and touching. Yes, they are a sign, whereas most of our buildings (sometimes even our churches) have no atmosphere, no soul. In some instances the attitude of the religious suffers. Many religious are unhappy because the buildings in which they live are vast and impersonal. Women belonging to congregations whose immense mother-houses can hold two or three hundred religious tell me of their sufferings. Everyone is unhappy: the religious, the superiors – the people in the neighbourhood, because they are scandalized and do not understand. To alter this state of affairs we must work out a bold and courageous solution. The changes and adaptations necessary if we are to make such buildings conform to, and give witness to, the Gospel, would, it is true, involve costly decisions. But we must realize that here spiritual values are at stake and that the expenditure would be off-set by a gain in promoting values which must be safe-guarded.

Again, on the level of the Church's institutions, poverty presents a serious and complex problem. And by institution I mean all organizations associated with the administration of the Church: they can be concerned with the apostolate or the diocese or charitable works or education at every level. The up-keep of these often involves enormous sums of money. Even on the modest plane of a parish the problem arises. I know a priest who was so weighed down throughout an entire year by anxiety in raising the money necessary for the up-keep of two schools that, as a result, he had neither the time nor the heart to occupy himself with his pastoral ministry. Problems of this kind are innumerable in all countries. The thought of the anxiety and the time that priests and religious have to devote in the world to these questions of administration and finance is enough to dis-may and scandalize anyone. A situation of this kind cannot indeed suddenly be altered without careful thought, but too many persons are asking why the Church itself does not face the problem. It is more and more necessary that the Church should be presented as having nothing to give other than Jesus Christ. 'I have neither gold nor silver; but what I have, this I give you,' Peter said to the man who asked him for alms. Moreover almost everywhere there is an increasing trend in this direction among priests and relig-ious who are concerned for the kingdom of God.

The Church, however, will always need resources. The question is how are these to be procured. I remember having in my hands a Marxist journal, intellectual in tone, which contained an historical study of the states belonging to the Church and also the Vatican as it is today. This article described the organization of the Church with a juridical and historical exactness that was remarkable. As long as the author confined himself to the sphere of history, all he said was flawless. His tone was even one of admiration: he praised the excellence and wisdom shown in the organization of the Church as a society. But he went on to say that, since the Church was a non-productive society, it could not survive of itself and consequently had to derive its resources from capital. This meant, he concluded, that the Church could not survive in a socialist régime, and must, therefore, be opposed to all evolution along socialist lines, under pain of pledging itself to its own ruin. The Church, indeed, in the view of the author, provides one of the greatest obstacles to the evolution of human society. The analysis provided by this Marxist historian was – granting his premises – entirely convincing. And this is what is felt in a confused kind of way, *en masse*, by the workers.

The Church will be required, increasingly, to give proof – not only by repeated affirmations, but by its actions and economic attitudes – that it is independent of money and consequently able to survive in régimes other than those based on capitalism. A greater poverty and simplicity in the ways used in spreading the Gospel, as well as in the Church's institutions, should enable the Church to find better means of balancing its budget by the help of a voluntary, enlightened collabortion on the part of the faithful as a whole: the laity should, indeed, be enabled to see this collaboration as coming within the scope of a Christian's duty. But this participation of the faithful at all levels, from the needs of the parish to those of the universal Church, cannot be achieved unless Christians are made aware of the need for these resources and are told, as far as is possible, to what use their contributions are being put. This openness in the deploying of the Church's resources and the use to which they are put will become indispensable if the spiritual mission of the Church is to be apparent to all – so that Christians, in peace and confidence, and in a spirit of generosity can, in full collaboration with the hierarchy, share in the material responsibility of spreading the Gospel throughout the world.

*

Now a word about poverty in relation to the means to be employed by the apostolate in making known the Gospel message. Some of these are costly, others less so. The expenses incurred by Saint Paul and the Apostles in accomplishing their mission were limited: all they wanted was enough to support them and enable them to travel from place to place. Indeed the problem raised by heavy costs has emerged above all during the last fifty years. Today the financial requirements of some missions are considerable: they include the organization of world congresses, modern methods of communication, motor vehicles, radio stations, even aeroplanes. In some countries all this involves enormous expenditure. Where does it end – for the Church or the Christian community has to pay? And, as a rule, these missions are established in countries that are poor. The moment will come when a decision as to our policy will have to be made. In the last analysis does not the apostolate, in the strict sense of the word – leaving aside means it may call to its aid – amount to an immediate, living contact with the apostle as he proclaims the Lord in the most direct way possible, while giving witness, by his manner of life, to the message which he brings?

Material means are useful. Perhaps they appear necessary. But they are always dangerous, and are a burden imposed on the preaching of the Gospel. The sense of the expression 'poor means' is not easy to define, and we should use it with caution. However, we could say that it is a matter of those means which by their very nature correspond to the Gospel message. Yes 'poor means' are those particularly suited to passing on the message without distortion.

*

I cannot end without reverting to what I mentioned at the beginning: the need for harmony and mutual under-standing between the messenger of the Gospel and the poor – so that the poor may have the Gospel preached to them in the true sense of the word. The solution of this problem depends, I repeat, on a change of outlook and, I would go so far as to say, a change of sensibility – this being determined by the attitude adopted by the Church on questions that come within the range of its teaching. What line, for example, are we to take concerning régimes based on a socialist ideology? And, in developing countries, what line [are we to take in the world of the poor and the workers, whose aspirations are directed increasingly and irreversibly towards the establishment of genuine socialism. We should study very seriously, both urgently and realist-ically, the questions raised by the different kinds of social-ism. It is, I am well aware, a grave problem. The majority of the socialistic régimes, it must be admitted, rest upon a materialistic philosophy, if not a militant atheism. It is an undeniable fact that in our times those who intend to spread the Gospel will have to face a youth that has been moulded in the conviction that the non-existence of God is proved scientifically. But side by side with this there has been valuable research and experimentation on the plane of a sound, natural education, a genuine selflessness; a con-cern for the common good, and a refusal to allow human relationships to be based solely on motives of profit.

The youth of today are, as a whole, orientated towards a new type of society and a radically different conception of life – one in which God is irrelevant. Apostles, priests and missionaries who have anything to do with the young or the masses of the poor simply cannot afford to ignore this problem, unless they are going to abandon the preaching of the Gospel or maintain that it is impossible for it to be preached in the modern world.

There is hope offered by the Church, but the goal of this hope does not belong to this world. There is hope, too, among the workers, the masses, who think they can attain well-being immediately, here below. The two ends are not consistent, but we ask the Church, we beg the Church, at least not to stand in the way of this search for material betterment – rather to work, with man, for its establishment, in one shape or form. It would be vain to think that the Church here on earth can be, in all, more than the small number made up of those who believe in eternal life and in a personal God. If Christians are rejected by certain totalitarian régimes, this should be solely on account of their belief in God, and not for political reasons which have nothing to do with their faith. In conflicts of this kind all is far from being clear. Attitudes rooted in the past are slow to change. But we should take the initiative, and enquiring laymen should be in a position to search for right solutions in the form of an authentic socialism. Today, the preaching of the Gospel is impossible if it is divorced from these important problems that concern all mankind.

*

To conclude, I repeat that this problem of poverty of the Church is a difficult one. For we must have a realistic view of the world and the conditions in which the Church lives. Also, if we are to preserve peace we must set to work courageously, knowing clearly what we are doing. The danger lies in our thinking that the problem can gradually resolve itself as time goes on. Furthermore, we must face the fact that it cannot be completely solved as we would wish. To understand this we have only to glance over the history of the Church, as well as listen to the demands made upon it in our own times. In a world where faith in God is shaken to the foundations, where Christians have lost their bearing, so that they have difficulty in keeping intact their belief in a living, personal God and in his Son Jesus Christ – it is in this world that the Church must be completely renewed, while at the same time remaining itself – remaining, too, a sign of contradiction.

The task of approaching the world of the poor is difficult. I have many times felt incapable of giving concrete advice to bishops or priests who asked me what they should do to make the Church the 'Church of the Poor'. If we can see the direction in which we must move, the solutions vary from place to place, for we are all of us human beings, whose ways of thinking differ. We churchmen are involved, along with our fellow countrymen, with different political régimes. We belong, also, to different cultures. Moreover our background and the education we have received have a much more profound influence on us than we think. But we must set to work with courage – (this is essential), telling ourselves that one generation on its own cannot bring about the rejuvenation that is necessary if the Church is to take stock, so that it can once again be capable of spreading the Gospel message among the poor.

Pope Paul's Address at the Closing of the Retreat

To try to make a brief summary of all that we have medi-
tated upon in the course of these days would be difficult,
probably impossible at this moment. However let me say
at once that the general impression left after the hours
spent in this chapel, during the last week, in silent meditation of all that was presented to us, has been (I speak,
I am sure, for everyone) a moving experience. In one
respect, indeed, it is easy to summarize, in that we all
of us take away a feeling of deep spiritual satisfaction and
inner joy – a sense of discovery.

This should give us food for thought, which is excellent.
We have spent our whole life trying to live in the service of
the Lord, trying to learn his teaching, penetrate his mysteries, live by his example. However, when we listen to the
episodes from the Gospel and the mysteries of the faith
that have been propounded to us, it is all too obvious that
we have a whole world still to discover. Ahead of us
stretches an endless vista hitherto unknown.

For that is how it is: *Caritas vestra magis ac magis abundet
in scientia et in omni sensu*. We have a duty to move forward:
to strive tirelessly to reach ever greater heights in our knowledge of Christ. We have a duty to test how fruitful has been
our effort to get to the heart of the Gospel teaching and the
doctrine of the Church in its surest and most authentic
expression. And as if that were not enough, we pass on to

another great discovery: that the knowledge of Christ we have acquired must be applied to all the concrete circumstances of our lives. We must try to see the complexity of the problems involved. They are, indeed, extremely complex: for they are profound, startling in their novelty, and demanding of an answer in the light which the growing knowledge of Christ will give to us. We must live faithfully by the Gospel, make our lives really conform to it. We may have thought we had already learnt to live by it; we may have thought we had already put it into practice, incorporated it into our lives as human beings. But, now, contact with the world around us, with harsh reality, with so much that is happening, shows us, on the contrary, that we have almost to begin all over again. Why is this? Because the Gospel is a source which never dries up. And since the world passes and changes, the relationship between the Gospel and the world, the Gospel and experience, the Gospel and the soul of each one of us, must be constantly renewed. Confronted with these two realities – Christ and the world – we are, by reason of this fact, called to a new formation, a new spiritual life: we have to acquaint ourselves with Christ, with the Gospel, and with our faith, in a manner which is indeed new and hitherto almost beyond our imaginings.

All this enables us to appreciate that during these last few days we have indeed been admitted to a deeper knowledge of Christ. We must therefore thank the preacher who so simply, yet with such profound insight and sincerity, has guided us on our way. Furthermore we ought to understand that a retreat of this kind, far from ending now, is, on the contrary, only beginning. We will genuinely profit from these days if, instead of letting the memory of them slip into the back of our minds among things that pass, we give it a place in the forefront of our consciousness as something to be put into practice, immediately, without loss of time, as if we had to begin all over again to remain faithful to the grace that God has bestowed on us during these days enriched by his blessing.

Let us first of all thank the Lord for his goodness in renewing his invitation to advance in holiness and dedication. Let us thank also the speaker. We should like no less to thank all those who have been present at this spiritual gathering. In short, we thank you all. We are confident that, helped by our efforts, our sacrifice, our example, the Church to which we all belong, whose mission is to make known in the world the life and the teaching of Christ, will grow to the greatest possible glory of God. May this occasion be one that is truly full of grace and promise of joys to come!

This is our sincere hope as we grant to all here present our Apostolic Blessing.